AF535051

ZAGATSURVEY

1995

SAN FRANCISCO BAY AREA RESTAURANTS

Edited by
Anthony Dias Blue

Coordinated by
Jack R. Weiner

Published and distributed by
ZAGATSURVEY
4 Columbus Circle
New York, New York 10019
212 977 6000

To

Margaret

and

Homer Surbeck

Acknowledgments

First and foremost, we want to thank the over 1,400 Bay Area restaurant-goers who took the time to fill out the questionnaire. This book is dedicated to their intelligence and their hearty appetites. Our special thanks also go to Vicki Bagrowski, Kathy Blue, Ted Cuzzillo, Maryalice Groves, Leroy Meshel, Jeff Petrick, Carol Seibert, Stephen Siegelman and Tammy Tang, and for their help. Naturally, we also want to express our gratitude to the chefs and restaurateurs who work so hard to make the Bay Area one of the most exciting culinary centers in the world. Thanks and *bon appétit*.

ISBN 1-57006-011-8

Contents

Introduction

Here are the results of our *1995 San Francisco Restaurant Survey* covering more than 550 restaurants in the San Francisco Bay Area from the wine country of Napa and Sonoma in the north to the verdant oceanside communities of Monterey and Carmel in the south. More than 1,400 people participated. Since they dined out an average of 3.1 times per week, this *Survey* is based on more than 230,000 meals per year.

By regularly surveying large numbers of local restaurant-goers, we think we have achieved a uniquely current and reliable guide. We hope you agree. On the assumption that most people want a "quick fix" on the places at which they are considering eating, we have tried to be concise and to provide handy indexes.

Knowing that the quality of this *Survey* is the direct result of their thoughtful voting and commentary, we sincerely thank each participant. They include numerous professionals, business executives and just plain folks – food lovers all.

We are most grateful to our editors, Anthony Dias Blue, the nationally syndicated food and wine radio and television commentator and columnist, and to his assistant, Jack Weiner.

We invite you to be a reviewer in our next *Survey*. To do so, simply send a stamped, self-addressed, business-size envelope to ZAGAT SURVEY, 4 Columbus Circle, New York, NY 10019 so that we may contact you. Each participant will receive a free copy of the next *San Francisco Bay Area Restaurant Survey* when it is published.

Your comments, suggestions and even criticisms of this *Survey* are also solicited. There is always room for improvement – with your help!

New York, New York
December 15, 1994

Nina and Tim Zagat

Foreword

This year's new *Survey* once again proves that San Francisco is a city that loves to eat. Diners have a critical attitude that embraces innovation, provided that it works. Don't try passing off trendy style over substance on the locals. Quality cooking is always appreciated and supported in the Bay Area. Take for example, Alain Rondelli's humbly adorned Richmond eatery. What this spot lacks in location and dressing, it makes up for with stunning French cuisine, and table reservations have been tougher to get than 50 yard-line seats for the Forty Niners.

An exciting group of young chefs, like Mr. Rondelli, are now vying for our palates, making a friendly challenge to the old guard. It was not long ago that upstarts like Alice Waters of Chez Panisse, Hubert Keller of Fleur de Lys, and Jeremiah Tower of Stars were redefining the Bay Area and national dining scene. Though vibrant as ever, these are *the establishment* restaurants, the yardsticks by which the latest crop of chefs measure themselves.

This past year was once again one of growth, where openings outpaced closings, and Bay Area dining became richer and more appealing than ever. Elka Gilmore, the highly creative chef of Elka Seafood Restaurant, is testing the Downtown waters with her highly anticipated Liberté. Meanwhile, across Market Street, Reed Hearon has managed to avoid the sophomore slump, expanding his remarkably successful LuLu Restaurant with an adjacent fixed-menu cafe, LuLuBis. Lest these upstarts grab all the headlines, Jeremiah Tower has kept busy by expanding his constellation with a larger, relocated Stars Cafe and the brand new Stars Oakville Cafe. Further bolstering the once-diluted wine country dining scene is Catahoula, where chef Jan Birnbaum gets back to his New Orleans roots in high style. The stars certainly came out for the opening of Rubicon, whose high-powered proprietors include Robert DeNiro, Robin Williams and Francis Ford Coppola. Finally, a late entrance into the mix is Bistro M, the latest piece in celebrity chef Michel Richard's collection that started with the renowned Citrus in Los Angeles.

Only a few closings stunt this season of growth. The trendy Etrusca has closed its doors, but before you turn the page in your Rolodex, you might want to write in the promising Eric Restaurant, which has taken its place. Downtown diners will no doubt mourn the departure of Geordy's, a slick and bustling spot that shown brightly before its rather sudden demise. But the chef is now holding forth at The Heights and Geordy himself is running Moptons.

Keeping pace with all these changes can be a daunting task, and that is why we rely on the witty and prescient comments of over 1,400 Bay Area surveyors. These reviewers love restaurants and eat out regularly. It is through their efforts that this *Survey* provides the most accurate (and we hope entertaining) guide to the Bay Area's expansive culinary landscape.

The trend in San Francisco is for people to eat out more frequently. With a large, young and mostly single population, the choice between home and dining out seems to be an easy one. Locals seem to be less concerned with cost than convenience, but they are still gravitating to more casual, less-expensive places and they still like to celebrate over a major meal at Masa's or the Ritz-Carlton Dining Room.

This is corroborated by the most encouraging trend of all: the average cost of a meal in the Bay Area has dropped by over nine percent since 1992. New restaurants tend to aim for midrange pricing and many of the existing eateries have scaled back their tabs by offering affordable fixed price menus. No doubt about it, it's a buyer's market when it comes to eating in the Bay Area this year.

San Francisco, CA
December 15, 1994

Anthony Dias Blue

Key to Ratings/Symbols

This sample entry identifies the various types of information contained in your Zagat Survey.

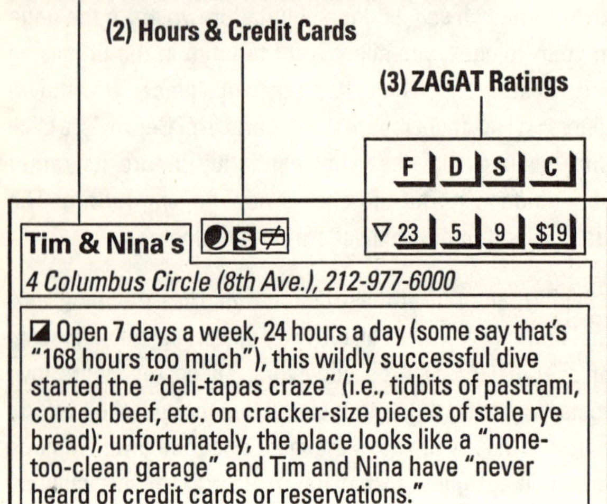

The names of restaurants with the highest overall ratings and greatest popularity are printed in **CAPITAL LETTERS**. Addresses and phone numbers are printed in *italics*.

(2) Hours & Credit Cards

After each restaurant name you will find the following courtesy information:

◐ .... *serving after 11 PM*

S .... *open on Sunday*

≠ .... *no credit cards accepted*

(3) ZAGAT Ratings

Food, Decor and **Service** are each rated on a scale of **0** to **30**:

F	D	S	C

F .... **Food**
D .... **Decor**
S .... **Service**
C .... **Cost**

23	5	9	$19

0 - 9 .... *poor to fair*
10 - 19 .... *good to very good*
20 - 25 .... *very good to excellent*
26 - 30 .... *extraordinary to perfection*

∇ 23	5	9	$19

∇ .... *Low number of votes/less reliable*

The **Cost (C)** column, reflects the estimated price of a dinner with one drink and tip. Lunch usually costs 25% less.

A restaurant listed without ratings is either an important **newcomer** or a popular **write-in**. The estimated cost, with one drink and tip, is indicated by the following symbols.

–	–	–	VE

I .... *below $15*
M .... *$16 to $30*
E .... *$31 to $50*
VE .... *$51 or more*

Occasionally, a restaurant's numerical ratings and comments are based on our *1994 Survey,* as indicated by a **(94)** following the restaurant's name.

(4) Surveyors' Commentary

Surveyors' comments are summarized, with literal comments shown in quotation marks. The following symbols indicate whether responses were mixed or uniform.

◪ .... *mixed*
■ .... *uniform*

Bay Area's Most Popular Restaurants*

Each of our reviewers has been asked to name his or her five favorite restaurants. The 40 spots most often named, in order of their popularity, are:

1. Postrio
2. Stars
3. Fleur de Lys
4. Masa's
5. Aqua
6. Boulevard
7. La Folie
8. Lark Creek Inn
9. Square One
10. LuLu Bis/Cafe/Rest.
11. Fringale
12. Tra Vigne/N
13. Chez Panisse
14. Cafe Chez Panisse
15. Ritz-Carlton Din. Rm.
16. Zuni Cafe
17. Greens
18. Elka
19. One Market
20. Alain Rondelli
21. Domaine Chandon/N
22. Moose's
23. Bix
24. Stars Cafe
25. Flying Saucer
26. Campton Place
27. Mustards Grill/N
28. Pane e Vino
29. Kuleto's Italian
30. Cypress Club
31. Hayes St. Grill
32. Fresh Cream/S
33. Lalime's
34. Cha Cha Cha's
35. Il Fornaio
36. Rist. Ecco
37. South Park Cafe
38. 231 Ellsworth
39. Bay Wolf
40. Acquerello

It's obvious that good things come at a price – most of these restaurants are also among the area's most expensive. Of course, San Franciscans also look for good value in their restaurants. Accordingly, we have listed over 100 "Best Buys" on pp. 18 and 19.

*All restaurants are in the San Francisco metropolitan area unless otherwise noted (N = North of San Francisco and S = South of San Francisco).

Top Ratings*

Top 40 Food Ranking

29 Masa's
Erna's House/S
Fleur de Lys
28 Ritz Carlton Din. Rm.
Emile's/S
Chez Panisse
Le Marquis
La Folie
Cafe Chez Panisse
Postrio
Terra/N
Domaine Chandon/N
Pacific's Edge/S
27 Stars
Aqua
French Laundry/N
Lark Creek Inn
Sherman House
Fresh Cream/S
Le Mouton Noir/S
Park Grill
Campton Place
Central 159/S
Silks
Acquerello
Fringale
Citron
231 Ellsworth
Kenwood/N
26 Helmand
Flying Saucer
Tra Vigne/N
Square One
Mustards Grill/N
Lalime's
Bay Wolf
Le Papillon/S
John Ash & Co./N
French Room, The
Woodward's Garden

Top Spots By Cuisine

Top American
27 Stars
French Laundry/N
Lark Creek Inn
Park Grill
Campton Place

Top Breakfast†
28 Downtown Bakery/N
26 Paolo's/S
25 Casa Aguila
Zuni Cafe
24 LuLuBis/Cafe/Rest.

Top Cafes
28 Cafe Chez Panisse
27 Stars
25 Vivande Porta Via
Zuni Cafe
24 LuLu Cafe

Top Californian
29 Erna's House/S
28 Ritz Carlton Din. Rm.
Chez Panisse
Cafe Chez Panisse
Postrio

Top Cantonese/Mandarin
25 Tommy Toy's
House of Nanking
23 Flower Lounge
Yuet Lee
Mandarin, The

Top Chinese
25 Tommy Toy's
House of Nanking
24 Ton Kiang
23 China Moon Cafe
Wu Kong

---

*Excluding restaurants with low voting.
†Other than hotels.

Top Continental
26 French Room, The
Covey, The/S
25 El Paseo
23 Dal Baffo
20 Cal. Culinary Acad.

Top Delis
25 Vivande Porta Via
19 Brother's Deli
Narsai's Cafe
18 Max's Opera Cafe
16 Saul's Deli

Top Dim Sum
25 Yank Sing
23 Flower Lounge
Harbor Village
Wu Kong
Mandarin, The

Top Eclectic
28 Terra/N
27 French Laundry/N
26 Flying Saucer
Square One
Woodward's Garden

Top Family Dining
28 Chez Panisse
Pacific's Edge/S
27 Lark Creek Inn
Sherman House
Park Grill

Top French Bistro
27 Fringale
25 Chez T.J.
Anjou
Cafe Jacqueline
24 South Park Cafe

Top French Classic
29 Fleur de Lys
27 Fresh Cream/S
231 Ellsworth
24 Ernie's
L'Olivier

Top French New
29 Masa's
Fleur de Lys
28 La Folie
Domaine Chandon/N
27 Sherman House

Top Hamburgers
23 Mo's Burgers
22 Doidge's
19 Fat Apple's
18 Balboa Cafe
16 Hamburger Mary's

Top Hotel Dining
29 Masa's/Vintage Ct.
28 Ritz-Carlton Din. Rm.
Postrio/Prescott
Pacific's Edge/S/Highlands Inn
27 Sherman House

Top Indian
24 North India
22 Maharani India
21 Appam
20 Indian Oven
Gaylord Indian

Top Northern Italian
27 Acquerello
25 Pane e Vino
Rist. Milano
24 Rist. Ecco
La Fiammetta

Top Southern Italian
25 Vivande Porta Via
22 Palermo/S
Caffe Macaroni
Tommaso's
21 Little Italy

Top Japanese
26 Kabuto Sushi
25 Ebisu
Kirala
23 Yoshida-Ya
21 Goro's Robato

Top Late Night
26 Regina's
25 Zuni Cafe
23 Izzy's Steak
Yuet lee
21 Korea House

Top Mediterranean
28 Chez Panisse
Cafe Chez Panisse
27 Aqua
26 Square One
Lalime's

Top Mexican

25 La Taqueria
Casa Aguila
24 La Cumbre
21 Guaymas
20 Cafe Marimba

Top Newcomers/Rated

27 Citron
26 Regina's
Zax
25 Rivoli
24 Rubicon

Newcomers/Unrated

Bistro M
Heights, The
Left Bank
Pazzia
Primo Patio Cafe

Top Oyster Bars

24 Swan Oyster Depot
21 PJ's Oyster Bed
19 Pacific Heights

Top People-Watching

28 Chez Panisse
Cafe Chez Panisse
Postrio
27 Stars
Park Grill

Top Pizza

28 Cafe Chez Panisse
Postrio
25 Zachary's
Vicolo Pizzeria
23 Pauline's Pizza

Top Seafood

27 Aqua
26 Elka
Hayes St. Grill
Ebisu
24 Swan Oyster Depot

Top Steakhouses

25 Eulipia/S
Harris'
24 House of Prime Rib
23 Vic Stewart's
Izzy's Steak

Top Sunday Brunch

29 Erna's House/S
28 Postrio
Pacific's Edge/S
27 Lark Creek Inn
Sherman House

Top Thai

26 Thep Phanom
Marnee Thai
24 Khan Toke Thai
Narai
Manora's Thai

Top Wild Cards

26 Helmand/Afghan
25 Greens/Vegetarian
24 Rice Table/Indonesian
Casa Madrona/Pac. Rim
23 Nan Yang/Burmese

Top Worth a Drive

29 Erna's House/S
Oakhurst
Campbell House/S
Campbell
28 Chez Renee/S
Aptos
Emile's/S
San Jose
Pacific's Edge/S
Carmel

Top 40 Decor Ranking

29 Garden Court
28 French Room, The
Ritz-Carlton Din. Rm.
Erna's House/S
Pacific's Edge/S
Act IV
Auberge du Soleil/N
Sherman House
Aqua
Fleur de Lys
Tra Vigne/N
Postrio
27 Campton Place
El Paseo/N
Casa Madrona/N
Domaine Chandon/N
Tourelle Cafe
Silks
Lark Creek Inn
Meadowood Rest./N
Cypress Club
Bridges
Bix
Terra/N
Chateau Souverain/N
Wente Bros.
26 Boulevard
John Ash & Co./N
Covey, The/S
Vic Stewart's
Carnelian Room
Ritz-Carlton Terr.
Big Four, The
ERIC Restaurant
Napa Valley Wine/N
Le Mouton Noir/S
Fournou's Ovens
Tommy Toy's
Caprice, The
Paolo's/S

Top Outdoor

Chez Renee/S
Domaine Chandon/N
Erna's House/S
French Laundry/N
Grille/N
Lark Creek Inn
Le Mouton Noir/N
Park Grill

Top Romantic

Act IV
Acquerello
Auberge du Soleil/N
Casa Madrona
Casanova/S
Chez Renee/S
Erna's House/S
Fleur de Lys
Fournou's Ovens
French Laundry/N
French Room, The
Meadowood Rest./N
Sierra Mar/S
Terra/N

Top Rooms

Aqua
Boulevard
Big Four, The
Campton Place
Cypress Club
Ernie's
Fleur de Lys
Fournou's Ovens
French Laundry/N
Garden Court
Lark Creek Inn
Madrona Manor/N
Park Grill
Postrio
Meadowood Rest./N
Ritz-Carlton Din. Rm.
Ritz-Carlton Terr.
Sherman House
Square One
Stars

Top Views

Alta Mira
Auberge du Soleil/N
Caprice, The
Carnelian Room
Casa Madrona/N
Cliff House, The
Domaine Chandon/N
Gaylord/Ghirardelli
Greens
Harbor Village
Horizons/N
Julius' Castle
Mandarin
McCormick & Kuleto's
Pacific's Edge/S
Meadowood Rest./N
Sam's Anchor Cafe
Splendido's
Victor's
Waterfront

Top 40 Service Ranking

29 Erna's House/S
28 Ritz-Carlton Din. Rm.
Masa's
Fleur de Lys
27 Le Marquis
Covey, The/S
Sherman House
Campton Place
26 Chez Panisse
La Folie
Silks
Fresh Cream/S
Domaine Chandon/N
Park Grill
Emile's/S
French Room, The
Le Mouton Noir/S
Pacific's Edge/S
Acquerello
French Laundry/N
Terra/N
Postrio
John Ash & Co./N
Anjou
25 Le Club
231 Ellsworth
El Paseo
Lark Creek Inn
Bay Wolf
Square One
Wente Bros.
Lalime's
Barbarossa
Cafe Chez Panisse
Ernie's
Auberge du Soleil/N
Alain Rondelli
24 Tommy Toy's
Ritz-Carlton Terr.
L'Olivier

Best Buys*

Top 50 Bangs For The Buck

This list reflects the best dining values in our *Survey*. It is produced by dividing the cost of a meal into the combined ratings for food, decor and service.

1. La Taqueria
2. La Cumbre
3. Caffe Greco
4. Dottie's Cafe
5. Mario's Bohemian
6. Trio Cafe
7. Mama's Royal Cafe
8. Bette's Oceanview
9. JoAnn's Cafe
10. Ti Couz
11. Mo's Burgers
12. Zachary's Pizza
13. ¡Wa-Ha-Ka!
14. Mifune
15. Cafe Fanny
16. San Francisco BBQ
17. Campo Santo
18. Dusit Thai
19. Sally's Cafe/Bkry.
20. Cafe Flore
21. Doidge's
22. Eric's Chinese
23. Long Life Vegi Hse.
24. Cha Cha Cha's
25. Roosevelt Tamale
26. Tu Lan
27. La Mediterranee
28. Fat Apple's
29. Marnee Thai
30. Cactus Cafe
31. Phnom Penh
32. Emerald Garden
33. Bill's Place
34. Mel's Drive-In
35. Vicolo Pizzeria
36. Khan Toke Thai
37. Brother's Deli
38. Cafe Claude
39. Hamburger Mary's
40. Kelly's on Trinity
41. JoAnn's B Street
42. Swan Oyster Depot
43. Angkor Wat
44. Gira Polli
45. Sears Fine Foods
46. Manora's Thai
47. Olive's Pizza
48. Thep Phanom
49. Yank Sing
50. Casa Aguila

*All restaurants are in the San Francisco metropolitan area unless otherwise noted (N = North of San Francisco and S = South of San Francisco).

Additional Good Values

(A bit more expensive, but worth every penny)

Asimakopoulos
Aux Delices
Blue Chalk Cafe
Bocce Cafe
Brandy Ho's
Cafe/All Seasons
Cafe Bastille
Cafe Marimba
Caffe Roma
Calif. Pizza Kit.
Cheer's Cafe
Chevys
Curbside Cafe
Delancey St.
Eleven Rist. & Bar
Ernesto's
Esperpento
Fountain Court
Golden Turtle
Goro's Robato
Hard Rock Cafe
Helmand
House of Nanking
Hunan
Island Cafe
La Traviata
Leticia's
Liberté
Los Gatos Brewing/S
Mandalay
Max's Diner
Max's Opera Cafe
Mescolanza
Mom Is Cooking
Mozarella di Bufala
Nan Yang
Narai
Narsai's Cafe
North Sea Village
Pacific Cafe
Pauline's Pizza
Plearn Thai
Royal Thai
Ruby's
Sanppo
Saul's Deli
Siam Cuisine
Station House
Suppenkuche
Tanuki
Tommy's Joynt
Ton Kiang
Tortola
Venezia

Areas covered in Directory

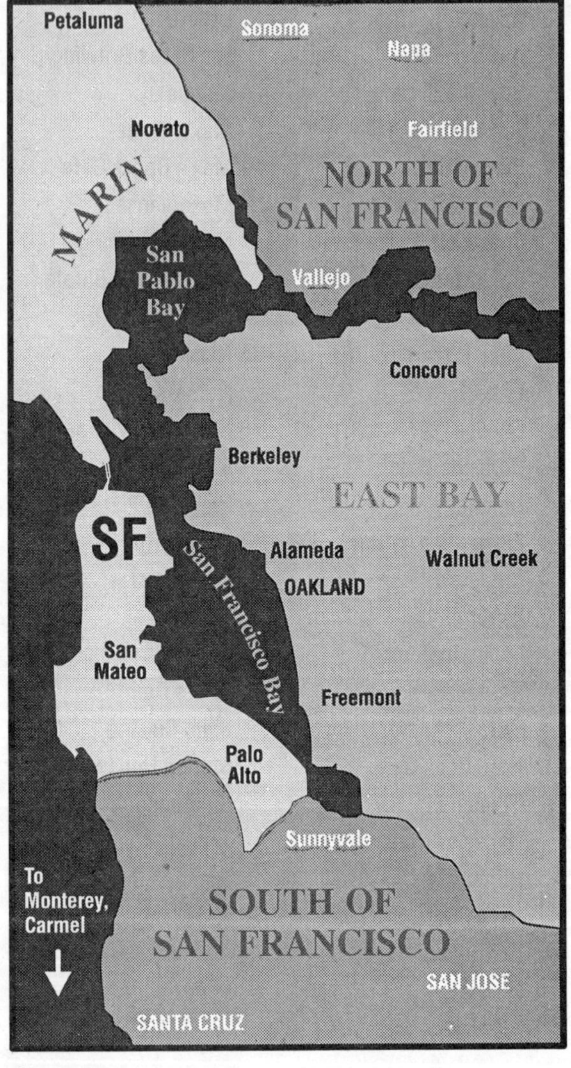

Alphabetical Directory of Restaurants

Abiquiu Restaurant S M 22 | 23 | 22 | $29

129 Ellis St. (Cyril Magnin), 415-392-5500

◪ John Sedlar's new, "very LA" Downtown eatery sizzles with his very individualistic, "fabulously presented" SW food: "terrific golden tamales", "interesting cactus dishes" and "the filet enchilada for my last meal"; tall prices for "lilliputian portions" put some off their feed, but most agree that this stylish place is "headed in the right direction."

Ace Cafe, The S M 16 | 16 | 15 | $17

1539 Folsom St. (bet. 11th & 12th Sts.), 415-621-4752

■ Happening SOMA "hangout" for those seeking low-budget, post-clubbing munchies; the Californian kitchen deals out "inventive" sandwiches and light food with "good music and feelings to go along"; despite just ok eats and "snotty service at times", this busy cafe is mostly coming up aces.

Acorn Tea & Griddle, The S 22 | 21 | 21 | $25

47 Powers St. (bet. 8th & 9th Sts.), 415-863-2469

■ Bright "oasis" in a shady SOMA environment that manages a "picturesque country-inn feel" complete with "lovely garden setting for brunch, lunch and tea"; this Acorn's "healthy", midpriced New American menu grows on vegetarians and nonvegetarians alike.

Acquerello 27 | 25 | 26 | $40

1722 Sacramento St. (bet. Polk & Van Ness Aves.), 415-567-5432

■ This "romantic, cozy" and "nontrendy" Van Ness/Polk Northern Italian gets high ratings for "refined" cooking with "intense flavors"; some find the menu "limited", but more agree it's "imaginative" and presents a "pleasurable dilemma"; a few say "haughty", but the majority gives kudos to the "gracious" host and "attentive, professional" staff.

ACT IV S M 22 | 28 | 24 | $38

Inn at the Opera, 333 Fulton St. (Franklin St.), 415-553-8100

◪ "Opulent decor" and "dark and romantic" ambiance co-star at this "jewel box" Civic Center French-Californian pre-/post-Opera; the majority rate the food and service "improved" from a year ago, although they "never match the setting" – "but looks ain't everything."

Adriana's S M 22 | 18 | 21 | $22

999 Andersen Dr. (Bellam St.), San Rafael, 415-454-8000

■ A strong local following praises Adriana Giramonte's robust "Classic Italian" cooking at this consistently "dependable" Marin "sleeper"; though the "warehouselike space with no charm" leaves some cold, reasonable prices warm them up.

Adriatic S 16 12 16 $22

1755 Polk St. (Washington St.), 415-771-4035

■ "Pleasant, simple" and "good for the price", this veteran seafooder's proximity to Van Ness makes it an "ok spot for lunch", and the fact that it's "average in every way" makes it not too hard to go back to the office afterward.

A La Carte S ▽ 18 16 19 $27

1453 Dwight Way (Sacramento St.), Berkeley, 510-548-2322

◪ If you long for a "real Paris neighborhood brasserie", try this "cozy, romantic" Berkeley French that serves "good food for the price"; admirers love "brunch" at this "longtime favorite", but the unsmitten say "just alright."

ALAIN RONDELLI S 25 19 25 $43

126 Clement St., (bet. 2nd & 3rd Aves.), 415-387-0408

◪ Chef Alain Rondelli's "cozy" New French storefront in the Richmond District has taken surveyors by storm: "sublime, honest French food without gimmicks" served by an "enthusiastic" staff; a few critics cite "bland" "Franco-Tudor" decor and "too rich" prices – but to get in you'd better call well in advance.

Alejandro's S M 17 14 16 $23

1840 Clement St. (bet. 19th & 20th Aves.), 415-668-1184

◪ This Spanish-Peruvian-Mexican in the Richmond District is described kindly as "down to earth," though some think the "shabby decor casts a pall over the meal"; aesthetics aside, "unique tapas" and "huge portions" of "consistently good paella" and Peruvian food outscore the "mediocre" Mexican menu; kitschy bonus: there's "festive" live music most nights.

Alexander Ristorante S M ▽ 21 20 20 $30

65 Moraga Way (Brookwood), Orinda, 510-253-1322

◪ Pasta and piano music draw locals to "eat frequently" at this "comfortable and warm" Northern Italian and give it generally good marks all around; the fact that it's "the only decent place" in upscale Orinda may explain what a few call "snobbish service" and an "overpriced" menu.

Alfred's Steakhouse S M 23 18 21 $31

886 Broadway (bet. Powell & Mason Sts.), 415-781-7058

■ "Time-warp" North Beach meat mecca where nostalgic carnivores come for that "old-time SF Italian feeling"; it's "what steakhouses used to be – red booths, red meat, red wine, big martinis" and "oooh that surf 'n' turf"; Alfred's army also savors the "excellent service from waiters as old and dusty as the building."

Alioto's Restaurant S M | 14 | 14 | 14 | $25 |

8 Fisherman's Wharf (Jefferson St.), 415-673-0183

◪ Wharf seafooder that traps tourists who come for "great waterfront views" and "not bad crab"; otherwise, the price is "high" for "average seafood"; "take your Midwest in-laws" and, if they're not in town, what would you be doing down here anyway?

Allegro S M | 21 | 17 | 22 | $29 |

1701 Jones St. (Broadway), 415-928-4002

■ This "cozy, friendly" Russian Hill Italian is like dining "at a friend's home"; neighborhood couples and "clandestine romantics" are regulars, but so are "intrusive politicos" doing the "power dinner" who at times spoil the "cheerful" atmosphere, though never the "great gnocchi."

Alta Mira Restaurant ◐ S M | 16 | 23 | 17 | $28 |

Alta Mira Hotel, 125 Bulkley Ave. (Princess), Sausalito, 415-332-1350

■ The raves are unanimous for the "fantastic view" of SF from the deck of this Marin Classic French, but surveyors also agree they have "never had anything decent to eat" in its slightly "rundown" dining room; "stop by for a cocktail, eat elsewhere" sums it up.

Amelio's S | 25 | 22 | 23 | $45 |

1630 Powell St. (bet. Green & Union Sts.), 415-397-4339

◪ Impressed surveyors gush over dining in this "stately home" in North Beach; a few feel that one could ask for less "stuffy service"; however, the Nouvelle French food is "always outstanding" even if "a bit out-of-date."

Angkor Wat S | 22 | 18 | 21 | $20 |

4217 Geary Blvd. (6th Ave.), 415-221-7887

■ With its "delicious" food ("the best warm beef salad" and "try the trout with mushrooms") and "entertaining" atmosphere (traditional dancers), this Richmond District Cambodian is "a nice change from the norm"; noticeable drawback is that "it's a bit cramped" and "starting to look like a basement rec room."

Anjou | 25 | 24 | 26 | $31 |

44 Campton Pl. (Stockton St.), 415-392-5373

■ Downtown French bistro that replaced the popular Janot, but retains its chef–co-owner, and most agree is "better than the original"; "generous servings" of "simple", "flavorful", French food by a "friendly", "energetic staff" in a "charming, crowded" setting is "what authentic bistro cuisine is all about."

Annabelle's S M | 17 | 16 | 16 | $23 |

68 Fourth St. (bet. Market & Mission Sts.), 415-777-1200

American grill near the Moscone Center that suits conventioneers, but most foodies find the fare "rarely better than fair"; it can produce "pretty good roast chicken" and grilled meats, but "flamboyant service" and only "adequate" other dishes make it "easy to get a table."

Appam Cuisine of Old India S M | 21 | 20 | 17 | $23 |

1261 Folsom St. (bet. 8th & 9th Sts.), 415-626-2798

"California-ized" Indian food that fans describe as "exciting, unique, creative" ("try unusual and good salmon in coconut milk and tandoori dishes"), but more traditional palates declare "not to my taste"; both sides agree that "service needs to relax."

AQUA M | 27 | 28 | 24 | $44 |

252 California St. (bet. Front & Battery Sts.), 415-956-9662

Hyperbole flows like nectar over this cosmopolitan Downtown Mediterranean that's "SF's best seafood restaurant"; chef George Morrone produces "dazzling food in a dazzling room" filled with large floral arrangements; some surveyors ask "is this a shrine or a restaurant?", but the vast majority "can't wait to go back."

A. Sabella's S M | 16 | 16 | 17 | $26 |

2766 Taylor St., 3rd Floor (Jefferson St.), 415-771-6775

"Can you say tourist trap?" asks one rhetorical critic about this Cal-Italian seafooder; more philosophical voices say "one of the safer bets in the Wharf area" (go for the chowder and fresh crab) and approve of the "good mystery dinner theater" and piano player, "informative staff" and, of course, the "lovely view."

Asimakopoulos Cafe S M | 21 | 15 | 19 | $19 |

288 Connecticut St. (18th St.), 415-552-8789

Potrero Hill Greek taverna that doesn't reach Olympian heights, but is "as good as Greek gets" in SF and "a value"; don't be put off by the tongue-twister name, just enjoy the tongue-teasing flavors and hearty, satisfying entrees; this "cute, little spot" in a "nice neighborhood" is worth the odyssey to get there.

Aux Delices M | 18 | 10 | 16 | $16 |

1002 Potrero Ave. (22nd St.), 415-285-3196

2327 Polk St. (bet. Green & Union Sts.), 415-928-4977 S

"Reliable but unexciting" French-Vietnamese fare in both Potrero Hill and Van Ness/Polk; fans delight in "tasty" appetizers and "crispy spicy chicken which is buried in the pork part of the menu."

Avalon S M | 18 | 22 | 19 | $29 |

639 E. Blithedale Ave. (Camino Alto), Mill Valley, 415-381-6284

◪ This Marin Hawaiian offshoot of a Maui original gets high marks for its "bustling" ("deafening") atmosphere and for its "adventuresome combinations" and "large selection of fresh fish"; but there's trouble in paradise – many object to "big hype" island-style, and to dishes that are "too sweet" and "overpriced."

Avenue Grill S M | 24 | 20 | 21 | $25 |

44 E. Blithedale Ave. (Sunnyside Ave.), Mill Valley, 415-388-6003

◪ "A hip, artsy crowd" favors this "friendly", "noisy" Marin grill as "a nice escape from the city" serving "good, solid" American food ("burgers and Caesars") at "reasonable prices"; "it's a good outing" with an "electric" atmosphere.

Bacco S M | 23 | 19 | 21 | $26 |

737 Diamond St. (24th St.), 415-282-4969

◪ "Long-awaited" Noe Valley Italian that's a "bit of Tuscany in the Happy Valley" with "delicious", "unusual entrees", "full-flavored" pastas and "tasty" meat dishes; this local trattoria has become "very popular" very quickly, but some find it "tragically hip."

Baci Caffe S M | 21 | 19 | 19 | $23 |

247 Shoreline Hwy. (Miller Ave.), Mill Valley, 415-381-2022

◪ Starters are standouts at this old-school Marin Italian, with "first-rate" antipasto and house-baked bread; some say that it goes downhill from there, with entrees that are only "satisfactory", but most agree it's still a "good value."

Bahia Restaurant S M | 15 | 15 | 14 | $21 |

41 Franklin St. (Lily St.), 415-626-3306

◪ Brazilian "hole-in-the-wall" off Market Street that's "good for the novelty experience" – dancing, live music, funky setting – "but after that wears off there's not much left"; the tropical cuisine varies from "ok to disappointing", and the same can be said for decor and service.

Baker St. Bistro S M | 22 | 14 | 23 | $23 |

2953 Baker St. (bet. Lombard & Greenwich Sts.), 415-931-1475

■ This diminutive Union Street "neighborhood delight" is described as a "phone booth with excellent French food"; "simple, fresh bistro fare", "good value", "très friendly service" and "warm" owners who are very "hands-on" make it elementary for locals to "return again and again."

Balboa Cafe S M | 18 | 16 | 17 | $20

3199 Fillmore St. (Greenwich St.), 415-921-3944

■ "Good, old Union Square standby" Californian that's "great for a martini and a burger"; also on the menu are celeb-watching and singles "action"; "charming, *Cheers*-like atmosphere" makes it "just right after a movie" or for a "Sunday brunch, football-on-TV kind of day."

Barbarossa M | 24 | 19 | 25 | $35

3003 El Camino Real (E. Selby Ln.), Redwood City, 415-369-2626

■ A "classic Italian-Continental with timeless preparations" that's "Redwood City's finest, whatever that means"; overall most find it "friendly" and "a cut above very good for food and service", but much depends on the "presence or absence of the chef-owner."

Bardelli's M | 14 | 15 | 18 | $24

243 O'Farrell St. (bet. Power & Mason Sts.), 415-982-0243

■ Venerable Downtown Northern Italian that some still find "soothing", especially for business lunch; the food is "pedestrian" and most agree that this survivor is "over the hill, way over" – and in SF that means something!

Barnaby's By The Bay S M | ▽ 15 | 20 | 15 | $20

12938 Sir Francis Drake Blvd. (Hwy. 1), Inverness, 415-669-1114

■ The bay's the thing – not the food – at this "simple, unpretentious" Marin BBQ seafooder on Tomales Bay; the "wonderful views" are fine for locals, but for everyone else it's "just too far to go."

Basta Pasta ◐ S M | 13 | 11 | 13 | $20

1268 Grant Ave. (Vallejo St.), 415-434-2248

◪ North Beach "pasta factory production line" serving "overcooked", "disappointing carbs" that "even lots of wine can't help"; it's also "tacky" and "too noisy" with "indifferent" service, yet "hordes" continue to drop by as it's a "convenient night-life option" in a "fun neighborhood" that "handles large groups well."

Bay Wolf Restaurant S M | 26 | 22 | 25 | $33

3853 Piedmont Ave. (Rio Vista), Oakland, 510-655-6004

■ Diners at this Californian-Mediterranean "pioneer" in North Oakland can't decide which meal is best: "huge" "satisfying" breakfast, "excellent" lunch on the patio or the "simple, yet elegant" dinner; the "interesting menu" "changes monthly" and they "treat you like you're special" at this "Bay Area treasure" that's worth howling about.

Bella Vista Restaurant M | 20 | 23 | 22 | $38

13451 Skyline Blvd. (south of I-92), Woodside, 415-851-1229

"Great views" justify "the long drive" to this Woodside Continental "mountain retreat"; the "much-improved" but "unimaginative" food doesn't reach any heights, though the prices do; it's the "romantic ambiance", "wonderful bar with fireplace" and "gorgeous" location that draw the crowds.

Bella Voce Ristorante & Bar S M | 17 | 21 | 21 | $28

Fairmont Hotel, 950 Mason St. (California St.), 415-772-5199

The waiters sing for your supper at this Nob Hill Italian, but things would be better if there was "more serving" to go with the singing; although the fare is "so-so" and "overpriced", the "nice atmosphere" and "concept" make it the "best birthday serenade anywhere"; N.B. there's a new chef, so stay tuned.

Benihana S M | 16 | 16 | 18 | $25

1737 Post St. (Webster St.), 415-563-4844
2074 Vallco Fashion Park (Hwy. 280, exit on Wolfe Rd.), Cupertino, 408-253-1221

"Playing with your food" takes on special meaning at this national-chain Japanese duo, where the grill chef's slice, dice and "chop-chopping" is an "entertaining floor show" for kids and cousins from Dubuque; once the "pseudo-Japanese fast food" is served, most critics decide that there's more flash than sustenance here.

Bette's Oceanview Diner S M | 23 | 16 | 17 | $14

1807 Fourth St. (Hearst Ave.), Berkeley, 510-644-3230

Everybody praises the "hearty breakfasts" at this "funky" but chic diner and – in the next breath – screams about the "90-minute waits" that prove "the human herd instinct"; even beyond the ocean view, word on this diner's "good eatin'" got out long ago.

Big Four, The S M | 23 | 26 | 24 | $36

Huntington Hotel, 1075 California St. (Taylor St.), 415-771-1140

This classic Nob Hill American is a "wonderful dinosaur" in a "beautiful, British gentlemen's-club" setting; all is "cozy and secure", and whether there for "power dining" or "intimate dining", the service impresses and the "traditional fare" is "superb", especially the "special game dinners."

Bill's Place S M | 15 | 7 | 13 | $11

2315 Clement St. (bet. 24th & 25th Aves.), 415-221-5262

For "a trip back in time" with "big, greasy burgers" served by "old doll" waitresses, try this "classic joint" in the Richmond District complete with outdoor garden; though "it's not just the food that's greasy", fans argue that with "the best patty melt in Christendom" and "great burgers, who cares about ambiance?"

Bistro Clovis M 21 | 17 | 19 | $22

1596 Market St. (Franklin St.), 415-864-0231

■ Civic Center French bistro that's a "nice pre-arts choice" with an "amiable look and feel, warm service and clever food"; a few complain about the "unchanging menu", but high marks go to the "lovely" lamb salad, "incredible" apple tart and "French wine sampler."

Bistro M S M – | – | – | M

Hotel Milano, 55 Fifth St. (bet. Market & Mission Sts.), 415-543-5554

Celebrated LA chef-restaurateur Michel Richard tests the Bay Area waters with this apricotty Downtown bistro; here, he keeps his French-accented Californian cuisine rustic and simple, featuring rotisserie entrees; the palm-bedecked interior includes a wall-sized mural of SF scenes.

Bix S M 24 | 27 | 22 | $34

56 Gold St. (bet. Jackson & Pacific Sts.), 415-433-6300

■ "Great martinis", "terrific" jazz and art deco "'20s supper-club decor" make this "ultra-stylish" Downtown American seem like a "movie set – you expect Bogart to come in any minute"; the menu is "dated" but "interesting and satisfying": chicken hash and filet mignon hit high notes and lobster pasta is a good riff; "it's the coolest for a night on the town" – but maybe a bit past its prime.

Bizou M 22 | 18 | 18 | $20

598 Fourth St. (Brannan St.), 415-543-2222

◪ Hip, new SOMA French-Italian bistro with "inventive" cooking and a somewhat "surprising menu", including "gutsy" beef cheeks, skate wings that "sparkle" and a highly touted string bean appetizer; though too noisy for a romantic dinner, it's a great place to see and be seen.

Blue Chalk Cafe S M 20 | 20 | 18 | $20

630 Ramona St. (bet. Hamilton & Forrest), Palo Alto, 415-326-1020

◪ Trendy Peninsula bar/restaurant/pool hall that serves soul-satisfying Southern cooking; unfortunately, the service often goes South as well; the later the hour, the more likely a "noisy, 20s, wanna-be crowd" will make an over-30 diner "feel like a grampa."

Blue Light, The S M 13 | 15 | 13 | $18

1979 Union St. (Buchanan St.), 415-567-4858

■ "Location and pool table are the redeeming factors" at this Union Street Cajun-Creole; while the "good bartender" may also be a plus, most agree the Light has been on the blink since owner Boz Scaggs left this "tacky", "young" and "loud" bar scene.

Bocce Cafe S M | 13 | 18 | 14 | $16
478 Green St. (Grant St.), 415-981-2044
◪ The reasons to go to this lively North Beach Italian are hearty portions, "value and atmosphere", but the "weak", "American-style Italian food" is best for "starving students and budget travelers" who don't mind "rushed service" and "mediocre pasta"; "large groups" agree that this Bocce is a ball.

Bonta S | 23 | 18 | 21 | $25
2223 Union St. (bet. Fillmore & Steiner Sts.), 415-929-0407
■ Small, small Union Street Italian that has a big, big following; goodness at this "incredible jewel" is the sum of "great service, food and atmosphere"; risottos and "some of the best pastas around" are highly recommended as is the vegetarian-friendly menu.

BOULEVARD S M | 26 | 26 | 24 | $38
1 Mission St. (Steuart St.), 415-543-6084
■ Hot, "high-style" SOMA New American combining the art nouveau decor of SF "King of Design" Pat Kuleto with "Queen of Cuisine" Nancy Oakes' hearty "Wolfgang Puck-meets-Betty Crocker" cookery; praise parades for the "glitz and glamour" and "beautifully presented" "big portions of exciting food."

Brandy Ho's on Broadway S M | 19 | 13 | 15 | $17
450 Broadway (Kearny St.), 415-362-6268
◪ This North Beach Hunanese offers "food hot enough to make your fingernails sweat – even the mild is hot"; ho-boy raves are for "fabulous" fried dumplings, "yummy" cold chicken salad and "really good" steamed fish; but "bring a flare gun to attract the waiters" and Formula 409 for the omnipresent grease.

Brasserie Savoy S | 23 | 22 | 21 | $31
Savoy Hotel, 580 Geary St. (Jones St.), 415-474-8686
◪ Bright, casual Downtown French that's "great for pre-theater dining and people-watching"; try the raw shellfish bar and "particularly good" seafood and grilled meats; "so many changes" in the kitchen and on the menu worry some, but others say the food is "constantly improving."

Bridges Restaurant & Bar S M | 25 | 27 | 24 | $36
44 Church St. (Hartz Ave.), Danville, 510-820-7200
■ "Casual" but "fashionable" Danville Californian that was a set for the movie *Mrs. Doubtfire*; on the far side of the tunnel, it's an "outpost of fine cooking" featuring "innovative", "carefully prepared" dishes with "quite a bit of Nouveau Japanese"; despite much praise, a few diners report the food can be "inconsistent."

Brother's Deli Restaurant S M 19 | 6 | 14 | $13

1351 Howard Ave. (El Camino Real), Burlingame, 415-343-2311

◪ It's not nearly New York, but this "no-frills" Chinese-owned Peninsula Jewish deli is the "closest thing locally" for "artery-clogging sandwiches" and chicken soup that cures colds and homesickness for the East Coast; mavens complain it's "a plastic deli" with a "dirty interior", but in an "area lacking authentic delis" this is "tops in its class."

Buca Giovanni 23 | 19 | 21 | $29

800 Greenwich St. (Columbus & Mason Sts.), 415-776-7766

■ "Reliable and unpretentious" North Beach Northern Italian with the "best selection of game in town", as well as "consistently good" veal and pasta; the "dark and musty" interior depresses some, but most "love the cave feeling", "friendly service" and "owner's presence."

Bucci's M ⊄ 21 | 19 | 18 | $23

6121 Hollis St. (bet. 59th & 61st Sts.), Emeryville, 510-547-4725

◪ The "alive atmosphere" at this "NY modern", "airy" place in Emeryville's warehouse area is just right for "first-rate pizza" and the "best Caesar salad in the East Bay"; service can range from "friendly, even after I tipped over my table" to "more Berkeley attitude."

Buchanan Grill, The S M 17 | 15 | 18 | $23

3653 Buchanan St. (bet. Bay & Northpoint Sts.), 415-346-8727

◪ "Comfy sports decor", "congenial bartenders" and "decent yuppie hamburgers" score points for this Union Street American; the home team calls it a "good joint", but blitzing critics sack it as an "uptight, sterile, pseudo sports bar" and say "my dog eats better."

Buckeye Roadhouse S M 24 | 24 | 22 | $28

15 Shoreline Hwy. (Hwys. 1 & 101), Mill Valley, 415-331-2600

■ Another winning way station on chef Cindy Pawlcyn's culinary trail (Mustards, Fog City Diner, Roti, et al); this "hunting lodge" with roaring fireplace has lots of "retro charm"; don't expect wild innovations – this is American "comfort food, not for the health-conscious": ribs, onion rings, "melt-in-your-mouth lamb shanks" and "lemon fries to die for" – "am I in heaven or just Marin?"

Buffalo Grill S M 23 | 23 | 20 | $27

Hillsdale Mall, 66 31st Ave. (El Camino Real), San Mateo, 415-358-8777

■ Trendy Peninsula American, with a Pat Kuleto–designed, "manly" Western motif, camping out in a shopping mall; the "solid, homestyle cooking" has suburban cowboys chowing down on "hearty portions" of game, steaks and pork chops that are "too heavy" for some but "just right, podnuh" for others.

Cacti Grill S M | 20 | 21 | 21 | $23 |

1200 Grant Ave. (2nd St.), Novato, 415-898-2234

◪ "It's yuppie Mex, but your mother would like it" at this "modestly priced" Southwesterner featuring a "varied menu" of pleasing but not dazzling foods served by a "helpful staff"; it's a best bet in Novato, where "there aren't many good places to eat."

Cactus Cafe & Taqueria S M | 21 | 13 | 15 | $15 |

393 Miller Ave. (LaGoma St.), Mill Valley, 415-388-8226

◪ The food is "healthy", "inexpensive" and "surprisingly good" at this Marin Cal-Mex cafeteria, making it an oasis for a quick lunch, dinner or refueling "after a bike ride"; regulars call it "a real treasure", but they're obviously talking about the food, not the decor or service.

Cadillac Bar & Restaurant S M | 14 | 14 | 15 | $19 |

1 Holland Ct. (bet. 4th & 5th Sts.), 415-543-8226

◪ Mediocre Mexican in a rowdy SOMA watering hole where tequila poppers fuel the action; the "noisy frat atmosphere" and "cheap gringo food" collide with eardrums and palates, but if you don't mind "big hair" and "college yups" and want to let loose at a "wild party scene", then park yourself here.

Cafe Adriano S | 24 | 21 | 22 | $29 |

3347 Fillmore St. (bet. Lombard & Chestnut Sts.), 415-474-4180

■ Past the "crummy entrance", you'll find a "smartly decorated", lively Marina cafe serving "consistently wonderful" Cal-Italian food; a few argue that the "menu looks better than the end result", but the same can't be said of the "extremely attractive", "very professional" staff; P.S. the early dinner is a "great buy."

Cafe Akimbo M | 20 | 19 | 19 | $22 |

116 Maiden Ln., 3rd Floor (bet. Grant & Stockton Sts.), 415-433-2288

■ This "hard-to-find" Downtown Californian in a former tearoom setting rewards the diligent with a "sunny, cheery lunch", "wonderful, unusual food" and "charming service"; popular with ladies who shop.

CAFE AT CHEZ PANISSE | 28 | 23 | 25 | $31 |

1517 Shattuck Ave. (bet. Cedar & Vine Sts.), Berkeley, 510-548-5049

■ Converts "wait in long lines" for this no-reserving, "budget Alice Waters" and claim this "upstairs cafe" is "even better" than her original Chez Panisse; like its parent, this "lovely" East Bay Mediterranean offers "extraordinary", "fresh" and "original" dishes from "top-rate ingredients", and "just as much attitude."

Cafe Bastille M 17 | 18 | 15 | $17

22 Belden Pl. (bet. Bush & Pine Sts.), 415-986-5673

◪ Downtown cafe with authentic French feel, including "brusque service"; it's "fun for business lunch" or allez to the alley after dark for "great live jazz" and "simple" bistro fare at "reasonable prices"; you can "sit outside on warm days."

Cafe Claude M 18 | 20 | 16 | $17

7 Claude Ln. (bet. Grant & Kearny Sts.), 415-392-3505

■ The waiters at this "cute" Downtown bistro may have "phony French accents", but the menu is "consistently good"; "wonderful specials", "good casual lunch" and "nice dinner jazz" attract the "trendy Gitane-smoking set."

Cafe de Bordeaux S M – | – | – | M

326 Seventh St. (Harrison St.), Oakland, 510-891-2338

"Cheap and delicious" Continental food is offered at this Oakland cafe (try the "excellent sizzling steak"); the people who run the place try to please – so why don't they rip out the awful decor and start again?

Cafe Fanny S M ⊄ 22 | 12 | 13 | $13

1603 San Pablo Ave. (Cedar St.), Berkeley, 510-524-5447

◪ This hyped-up "coffee stand" offers "great lattes" "served in a bowl", "good bread" and "exquisite apple turnovers"; however, some reviewers aren't keen on the rest of the experience, reporting "parking lot atmosphere" and an "arrogant attitude."

Cafe Flore S M ⊄ 16 | 17 | 12 | $12

2298 Market St. (16th St.), 415-621-8579

◪ A "people-watching mecca", this low-budget Castro Californian has "clientele as decor" and might better be called "Cafe Hair"; a "fun gay scene" offering "good breakfasts and lunch salads" and a "nice outside dining space", but beyond that only "mediocre" to "decent" food.

Cafe For All Seasons S M 21 | 15 | 20 | $21

150 West Portal Ave. (14th Ave.), 415-665-0900

50 E. Third Ave. (San Mateo Dr.), San Mateo, 415-348-4996

◪ "Crowded" Peninsula and Sunset American siblings that "emphasize freshness" in "simple, clean dishes"; they're "good for ladies who lunch" and "dependable after work", even though they could use "carpeting to warm the atmosphere" and dull "harsh echoes."

Cafe Jacqueline S 25 | 20 | 20 | $32

1454 Grant St. (bet. Green & Union Sts.), 415-981-5565

■ Ethereal, "melt-in-your-mouth soufflés" highlight this "cute" North Beach French "hideaway"; however, be prepared to bide your time for this "indulgent experience" since the soufflés – unlike the prices – "are slow to rise."

Cafe Kati S 24 | 20 | 24 | $32

1963 Sutter St. (bet. Fillmore & Webster Sts.), 415-775-7313

■ There's "art to eat" at this Pacific Heights Californian-Eclectic where "fabulous skyscraper presentations" are "as good as they look"; a few find the food "too fussy", but the majority appreciate "intensely personal cuisine" with service to match.

Cafe Maisonnette S 23 | 18 | 22 | $28

315 Eighth Ave. (bet. Geary & Clement Sts.), 415-387-7992

■ "Charming, postage-stamp cafe" in Richmond where the "family team" creates a "very personal, cheerful ambiance" and delivers "delicious French bistro cooking"; a few detractors feel it's "living on past reputation", but the intimate setting and "good food, good value" continue to attract a loyal following.

Cafe Majestic S M 21 | 25 | 23 | $34

Hotel Majestic, 1500 Sutter St. (Gough St.), 415-776-6400

◪ The Continental fare at this Van Ness hotel dining room, though very good, isn't as majestic as the ambiance, but it comes close, as does the "overworked but good staff"; a piano player-for-your-supper provides a "romantic tone" in a setting with "old-world charm" that appeals to "blue-haired ladies from the neighborhood."

Cafe Marimba S M 20 | 23 | 16 | $22

2317 Chestnut St. (bet. Scott & Divisadero Sts.), 415-776-1506

■ "At last, real Mexican regional cuisine", e.g., Oaxacan and Yucatan specialties, and – surprise, surprise – it's in the Marina; Reed Hearon (LuLu) hits pay dirt again with this "high-energy" cafe that's decorated like a Mexican marketplace and about as noisy; the staff struggles to keep up with the "lively, young crowd."

Cafe Mozart S 19 | 24 | 21 | $35

708 Bush St. (Powell St.), 415-391-8480

◪ "Romantic" Downtown Continental that may have slipped a notch or two with an ownership change; it still delivers "charm", "elegance" and "refined service", but "has lost some character with the new menu" that's pretty "pricey for a storefront location."

Cafe Riggio S M 20 | 17 | 18 | $23

4112 Geary Blvd. (5th Ave.), 415-221-2114

■ "Unpretentious" Richmond standby serving "straight-ahead Italian cooking at reasonable prices"; it's "plain but comfortable" with "friendly owners", "generous portions", "lots of oil and garlic" and "loud crowds" – all in all, an "ideal neighborhood haunt."

Cafe 222 S M ▽ 19 | 18 | 18 | $25

Hotel Nikko, 222 Mason St. (bet. Ellis & O'Farrell Sts.), 415-394-1100

◪ "Average" American food with Japanese touches is served by a "very capable staff" at this Downtown hotel dining room; most agree it's "good for breakfast meetings" when sleepy eyes won't notice the "sterile decor."

Caffe Delle Stelle M 23 | 16 | 20 | $22

330 Gough St. (Hayes St.), 415-252-1110

■ "Crowded but congenial" Civic Center 'caffe of the stars' that's at its frenzied best pre-arts, when the "authentic, hearty Italian" menu shines, as does the "*bella, bella*" staff; the tasty "cucina rustica" features "fantastic" salmon, pastas and a "leg of lamb special" at "bargain prices."

Caffe Greco S M ⊄ 17 | 19 | 16 | $11

423 Columbus Ave. (bet. Green & Vallejo Sts.), 415-397-6261

■ "Food is not the main feature" at this popular North Beach coffeehouse, but focaccia sandwiches and pastries play credible supporting roles to the "great coffees"; a "touch of Europe" that's "perfect for your morning cup or a snack."

Caffe Macaroni M ⊄ 22 | 13 | 19 | $25

59 Columbus Ave. (Jackson St.), 415-956-9737

◪ "Crowded", "funky" trattoria-style North Beach Southern Italian that most surveyors enjoy despite "low ceilings" and "somewhat high prices"; "go for the eggplant", "great antipasti and gnocchi."

Caffe Roma S M 14 | 17 | 12 | $15

414 Columbus St. (Vallejo St.), 415-391-8584

◪ "Classic" North Beach coffeehouse where "the food is a crime" and "naked cherubs frolic on the ceiling"; the staff is hardly angelic, but "frothy cappuccino" and "sinful tiramisu" are; for "good people-watching", "grab a window seat and enjoy life"; "don't miss the granita."

Caffe Sport ⊄ 18 | 15 | 9 | $26

574 Green St. (Columbus St.), 415-981-1251

◪ The rude waiters "should be fined for unsportsmanlike conduct" at this "tacky" North Beach Southern Italian where "abuse is part of the experience"; however, fans consider the "mounds of garlicky, cheap food" worth suffering for.

California Culinary Academy M 20 | 16 | 19 | $25

625 Polk St. (Turk St.), 415-771-3500

◪ Student cooking at this Civic Center American-Californian gets an "A for effort", but is "hit or miss" – depending on which class is in the kitchen, the food can be an "indulgent treat" or "like a salt lick"; the folks at the "huge" buffet clearly "want to be chefs not waiters."

California Pizza Kitchen S M 17 12 16 $16
438 Geary Blvd. (bet. Taylor & Mason Sts.), 415-563-8911
■ Glossy Downtown branch of Pepsi-owned pizzeria chain that bakes "unique topping combos" including Thai chicken or BBQ chicken on whole wheat crust; this "hassle-free choice" is "good for kids" and "convenient pre-theater", but wear sunglasses to fit in at this "very LA" eatery.

California Roastery M 18 12 15 $18
635 Clay St. (Montgomery St.), 415-956-1261
◪ Once a hot spot, this Downtown American-Continental has quickly cooled down; what is "wholesome", modestly priced food for some is "too greasy", "uninspired" and "predictable" for others; "the bloom is off this rose."

Campo Santo 19 22 15 $15
240 Columbus Ave. (Broadway), 415-433-9623
■ North Beach Mexican with "wild day-of-the-dead decor" that resembles a "Disney-designed Mexican graveyard"; despite "zombie-like" service, the "creative menu" is very much alive, however, thanks to "imaginative, healthy dishes" and "very fresh ingredients" at affordable prices.

Campton Place S M 27 27 27 $45
Campton Place Hotel, 340 Stockton St. (Sutter St.), 415-955-5555
■ While fans shed tears over the departure of chef Jan Birnbaum, the new kitchen team at this "serene", "top-dollar" Downtown American hit the ground running with "exquisite food" and "top-notch service" in a "very Eastern" formal setting; "fickle trend-chasers have moved on", but they've left behind a "quiet refuge of good taste" for the "establishment clientele."

Capellini 20 24 18 $28
310 Baldwin Ave. (B St.), San Mateo, 415-348-2296
◪ The "impressive Kuleto interior on three levels" at this "busy, noisy" Peninsula Italian gets bravos, but there's ongoing debate about the cucina; some praise the "satisfying food with a flair" and "large portions", but others insist the "Italian food is by imposters", the "pasta isn't up to par" and the waiters are "insolent" to boot.

Capp's Corner S M 15 13 16 $17
1600 Powell St. (Green St.), 415-989-2589
■ Family-style, "kick-off-your-shoes" North Beach "joint" where everyone feeds till full on tons of affordable, "hearty" though "uninspired" Italian; not haute but homey and "just plain fun", this "old-timer" "should be around a long time."

Caprice, The S M | 19 | 26 | 22 | $30

2000 Paradise Dr. (Mar West St.), Tiburon, 415-435-3400

◪ While many agree that "the food has improved" at this Marin Californian–New American under chef Kirk Byers, most still feel the "sweeping views of the City and Golden Gate Bridge" are "more memorable than dinner" – so securing a window seat is essential.

Caribbean Zone S M | 14 | 23 | 16 | $21

55 Natoma St. (bet. 1st & 2nd Sts.), 415-541-9465

◪ "When in an umbrella-in-your-drink mood" swing by this SOMA Caribbean; the "kooky island decor" includes indoor waterfalls and a "bar in an airplane"; the "fly-by-night food" often crashes, but it's "fun for cocktails after work" and "teenagers love the place."

Carnelian Room, The S M | 19 | 26 | 23 | $39

Bank of America Ctr., 555 California St., 52nd fl. (bet. Montgomery & Kearny Sts.), 415-433-7500

◪ Check out the "breathtaking view" from this "elegant" Downtown American atop the Bank of America building; the food doesn't reach such lofty heights, but "romantic atmosphere and scenery" make it worth the elevator trip even though prices can go "through the roof."

Carrara's Cafe M | ▽ 18 | 14 | 13 | $13

1290 Powell St. (Doyle St.), Emeryville, 510-547-6763

◪ The art on the walls may change, but not the fare at this old-style Italian-American, a "casual and comfortable" "neighborhood place" where you can "eat cheaply" and come away satisfied; there's plenty of praise for the polenta, but none for the service.

Casa Aguila S M | 25 | 14 | 18 | $19

1240 Noriega Ave. (19th Ave.), 415-661-5593

■ "Joyous" Sunset hole-in-the-wall that takes wing with "huge portions of interesting Mexican" food; a "bright, festive feel" complements "food with a flair", especially "great seafood dishes" and "always enjoyable" regional specialties; you won't go away hungry.

Casa Madrona S M | 24 | 27 | 23 | $34

801 Bridgeway Ave., Sausalito, 415-331-5888

■ A "world-class view" of Sausalito and the bay sets the mood at this "romantic" Marin hilltop serving "good", sometimes "great" Pacific Rim cuisine; though a few critics say the "quality varies", it's hard to resist the "sunset" and the "best weekend brunch for miles."

Castagnola's S M ▽ 17 | 15 | 17 | $21

286 Jefferson St. (Fisherman's Wharf), 415-776-5015

"Unremarkable but ok for the Wharf", this oldtime Italian seafooder traps tourists who come looking at lunchtime for "good cioppino" and a peek at the resident sea lions; anyone sniffing for more than "routine fish" is on the wrong pier.

Cava 555 M 18 | 20 | 16 | $26

555 Second St. (bet. Brannan & Bryant Sts.), 415-543-CAVA

"Sleek and sexy" SOMA room with an "impressive list" of Champagnes by the glass and live jazz that's a "great place to impress a date"; "more of a club than restaurant", its Californian menu is "good for grazing"; but try not to pop your cork at the "snooty maitre d'."

Cha Cha Cha's S M 24 | 22 | 17 | $18

1805 Haight St. (Shrader St.), 415-386-5758

"Hip and unusual" Haight place that delivers "spicy, flavorful Caribbean cooking" with "exotic treats" of "fried everything" to be cooled down with "super sangria"; the "festive" setting feels "like being in a giant pinata"; despite a new, larger location, "no reserving" means you can't cha cha in without a wait.

Chambord S M 19 | 17 | 19 | $26

150 Kearny St. (Sutter St.), 415-434-3688

"Civilized" and "dependable" Downtown French bistro, whose convenient location makes it a great spot to "do" breakfast but "a bit too crowded" at business lunch; critics feel the "food can be improved" and they "wish it would find a personality."

Cheer's Cafe S M 17 | 14 | 18 | $17

127 Clement St. (bet. 2nd & 3rd Aves.), 415-387-6966

Richmond neighborhood spot serving "good breakfast and lunch on the patio"; nothing on the "standard" American menu is out of the norm, but for "straightforward family dining" there are "better-than-you'd-expect" French toast, pizzas and salads.

Chevys S M 16 | 14 | 17 | $17

150 Fourth St. (Howard St.), 415-543-8060

650 Ellinwood Way (Contracosta Blvd.), Pleasant Hill, 510-685-6651

302 Bon Air Shopping Ctr. (Sir Francis Drake), Greenbrae, 415-461-3203

The weak link in this popular Mexican chain's "formula" is the Tex-Mex fare that's "blandized" "for the gringo palate"; however, the assembly line also delivers "cheery, quick service", a "good environment for kids" and chips and fajitas that live up to the 'Fresh-Mex' claims.

Chez Michel S | – | – | – | M

804 North Point St. (Hyde St.), 415-775-7036
A welcome Wharf revival, this charming French bistro has been scaled down and is now dressed in '90s garb with blond ash wood, tall windows and chrome bar trim; try the silky duck terrine, crab and spinach galette and French farm cheeses; attentive service adds to *la différence.*

CHEZ PANISSE S | 28 | 24 | 26 | $55

1517 Shattuck Ave. (Vine St.), Berkeley, 510-548-5525
◪ Everyone says that Alice Waters "invented California cuisine" here, but she says she's cooking Mediterranean; either way, most consider meals at this Berkeley shrine a "sacrament" leading to an "accessible heaven" where "freshest ingredients" produce "purest flavors"; a few agnostics "refuse to genuflect" saying the fixed, no-substitutions dinner is "Russian roulette" at these prices.

Chez T.J. | 25 | 23 | 24 | $50

938 Villa St. (Castro St.), Mountain View, 415-964-7466
◪ Peninsula Contemporary French located in a "wonderful redone Victorian"; the menu changes every two weeks, but the high food rating means it hits home most of the time; a few reviewers find it "pretentious all around and overpriced", but the majority roll with the "attitude" and enthuse over this "special place for romantic interludes."

China House Bistro S M | 23 | 19 | 20 | $26

501 Balboa St. (6th Ave.), 415-752-2802
◪ Shanghai-style surprises stir the "intriguing" menu at this "refined" Richmond spot where "chatty owners" welcome you into a stylish interior adorned with hanging murals from the 1930s; if the chef is "on" expect "great smoked duck" and "unique Chinese specialties", if he's "off" it's "like eating Chinese food in Arizona."

China Moon Cafe S M | 23 | 16 | 20 | $29

639 Post St. (bet. Jones & Taylor Sts.), 415-775-4789
◪ Barbara Tropp's high-concept Downtown "Asian diner" inspires a loyal following of "Troppezoids" who crowd in for "nicely presented, flavorful" "Chinese with a California twist"; critics cite uncomfortable cafeteria benches as "tough on the back" and the hefty bill as hard to stomach.

CIAO RISTORANTE S M | 20 | 20 | 19 | $24

230 Jackson St. (bet. Battery & Front Sts.), 415-982-9500
◪ Recently refreshed Downtown Northern Italian that has "staying power" thanks to "reliable, clean pastas", "delicious salads" and "creative appetizers"; a few claim "it's out of date" and "too bright and slick", but the majority say "it always feels good" to meet, greet and eat at this "consistent performer."

Citron S M — 27 | 21 | 24 | $33

5484 College Ave. (Taft St.), Oakland, 510-653-5484

■ There's a lot of buzz already about this "outstanding" new Oakland Contemporary French bistro serving "lovely", "earthy" fare; many say it's "what Chez Panisse used to be", but a few complain that there's "not much atmosphere" and service is not the greatest – "don't rush, they won't."

City of Paris S M — 21 | 20 | 20 | $26

Shannon Court Hotel, 101 Shannon Alley (Geary St.), 415-441-4442

■ "Happening" Downtown French with "delicious, hearty bistro cooking" at non-Parisian prices; it's "consistently fine" for "anything from hamburger to rack of lamb", with "magnifique roast chicken" for good measure; service can get "chaotic" in the "bustling, noisy" room, but it's a "good choice for late-night suppers or pre-theater."

Clark's by the Bay S M — 13 | 17 | 15 | $25

487 Seaport Ct. (Seaport Blvd.), Redwood City, 415-367-9222

◪ "If you're a sports fan", this Peninsula American owned by 49er legend Dwight Clark can be "fun"; however, most agree it drops the ball when the "so-so" food arrives; still, "friendly service" and "the chance to see a celebrity" pack them in; nonjocks may want to pass.

Clement Street Bar & Grill S — 19 | 15 | 19 | $20

708 Clement St. (8th Ave.), 415-386-2200

■ "Comfy neighborhood tavern" in Richmond that turns out "well-prepared", "basic fare" at "reasonable prices" – "dependably good" salads, burgers, pastas, soups and a "steak sandwich that's a steal"; a fireplace warms the "dark" but "relaxing" room; simplicity is a virtue here, so avoid complex menu items.

Cliff House, The S M — 12 | 19 | 14 | $25

1090 Point Lobos Ave. (Geary St.), 415-386-3330

◪ This "historic" Richmond American perched on the edge of the Pacific has "great sunsets" and "stunning ocean views, if it's not foggy", but sadly a "dreadful menu that's stuck in the 1950s" – only the "good omelets and popovers" don't nosedive; as for decor: the good news is they redecorated, the bad news is it "now looks like an Elks Banquet Hall in New Jersey."

Club 181 S — 20 | 20 | 16 | $25

181 Eddy St. (Taylor St.), 415-673-8181

■ "Groovy" Downtown American with "retro '30s decor" and "good but noninventive food" is "fun for groups" thanks to its "very hip" supper club atmosphere, "good live jazz" and billiards room; if you've got night fever "stick around for dancing", just be careful afterward in the "sketchy 'hood."

Cordon Bleu Vietnamese S ⌀ ▽ | 19 | 8 | 17 | $13
1574 California St. (Polk St.), 415-673-5637
"A one-dish wonder", this "dirt-cheap" Van Ness/Polk Vietnamese rates a medal from surveyors for its "fantastic five-spice chicken", but many other entrees, and the decor, are "too greasy"; still, if you're in the neighborhood, it's good for a "quickie meal pre-movie."

Courtyard Bar & Grill S M | 17 | 16 | 17 | $23
2436 Clement St. (bet. 25th & 26th Aves.), 415-387-7616
Richmond Cal–New American that has reviewers coming back for its "delicious cornbread", "nice neighborhood setting" and "generous food"; those who don't return cite "untrained staff" and a "constantly changing chef and menu"; nevertheless, "a good place to linger over lunch."

Crustacean S M | 21 | 17 | 17 | $27
1475 Polk St. (California St.), 415-776-2722
This Van Ness/Polk seafooder serves "erotically good" roast crab and garlic noodles, that may be "the best single dish in SF", and "superb drunken crab"; but other dishes aren't all they're cracked up to be.

Curbside Cafe S M | 18 | 12 | 18 | $17
2417 California St. (bet. Fillmore & Steiner Sts.), 415-929-9030
"Cramped" Pacific Heights Californian that's a "nice place to do brunch" and "watch the passing parade outside"; the "slowest chef in the west" takes his time to prepare "no-frills, but surprisingly ok food"; maybe "not a destination spot", but it's "reliable" for "casual neighborhood meals" and "good box lunches to go."

Cypress Club S M | 24 | 27 | 23 | $38
500 Jackson St. (Columbus St.), 415-296-8555
"Hello Dali" should be the theme song at this "plushly surreal" Downtown New American where "the food is quite good"; "don't worry, it's not your medication", the "wild" decor really looks "like sitting under a cow's udder during an acid trip"; the Eclectic fare "does a good job against the setting" (try the lobster soufflé), and "accommodating service" makes it easier to come feed and feast your eyes on this "trendy Wonderland."

Dal Baffo M | 23 | 21 | 23 | $43
878 Santa Cruz Ave. (University Dr.), Menlo Park, 415-325-1588
The "haute suburban" experience lives at this old-school Peninsula Italian-Continental; a few critics feel "the magic is gone now that the owner doesn't cook", but the majority agree the "traditional menu" still has a few tricks up its sleeve; however, the "excellent wine list", "elegant service" and "posh setting" don't come cheap, and some find the place "stuffy and pretentious."

Delancey St. Restaurant S | 19 | 19 | 21 | $21

600 Embarcadero (Brannan St.), 415-512-5179

■ "Assuage your PC guilt" at this SOMA American that boasts "good, hearty fare" at "fair prices" and "the friendliest service in town" by a staff of ex-cons and substance abusers trying to get back on track; here's "a social program that is working and tastes good too."

Doidge's S M | 22 | 13 | 18 | $15

2217 Union St. (bet. Fillmore & Steiner Sts.), 415-921-2149

■ Union Street American that belongs in the "Breakfast Hall of Fame" for its magnificent morning meals; "French toast is a star" with "superb eggs Benedict and corned beef hash" not far behind; expect to wait even with reservations, and, good grub aside, the "tired decor" could use some "new paint and carpeting, puh-leeze."

Dottie's True Blue Cafe S M ⊄ | 21 | 14 | 20 | $12

522 Jones St. (bet. Geary & O'Farrell Sts.), 415-885-2767

■ "Start your day with a smile" and a "respectable, creative breakfast" at this friendly Downtown diner; affordable "homemade food, fresh-baked bread" and true-blue service make it "like eating at mom's."

Doug's BBQ S M | 19 | 2 | 9 | $12

3600 San Pablo Ave. (36th St.), Emeryville, 510-655-9048

◪ Another candidate for "the best 'que around", this East Bayer offers "superb Soul Food"; fans advise "get their goat", "great ribs" and "try the turkey" – but "watch out for the hot sauce"; and don't even look for a table, there are none; this is strictly grab and go on the cheap.

Dusit Thai S M | 24 | 13 | 21 | $16

3221 Mission St. (Valencia St.), 415-826-4639

■ Hole-in-the-wall Mission gem with hole-in-one "spicy Thai food"; an "outstanding chef" turns out "unexpectedly excellent dishes", and the "pleasant staff" makes sure you get what you want; the "poor location" is the reason there's "usually no wait."

Ebisu M | 25 | 14 | 20 | $24

1283 Ninth Ave. (Irving St.), 415-566-1770

■ Richmond Japanese seafooder boasting "the most imaginative sushi in town" with "exotic" creations like the "caterpillar" maki roll; nonsushi dishes can be less predictable ("oily tempura"), but "friendly chefs" and "boisterous, interactive eating" make for large crowds and "long waits" at this "ultimate sushi bar."

Eddie Rickenbacker's M | 15 | 17 | 16 | $20 |

133 Second St. (Minna St.), 415-543-3498

◪ Motorcycles hang from the walls of this "crowded and noisy" SOMA American bistro that's a "glorified cafeteria for young lawyers"; watch legal eagles swoop down on "great big burgers" and "good Caesar salads" at this "popular after-work hangout", where the service seems to retire early as well.

Edokko S | – | – | – | M |

2215 San Pablo Ave. (Old Stone Way), Berkeley, 510-841-9505

Things are improving at this "homestyle" Japanese: this year, no one said an unkind word about the food, though "quite pleased with everything" was as good as it got; it also "needs a face-lift", so for visual interest check out the "great samurai helmet collection."

Eleven Ristorante & Bar M | 22 | 22 | 21 | $23 |

374 Eleventh St. (bet. Folsom & Harrison Sts.), 415-431-3337

◪ A new translation of the once-trendy Undici restaurant, this "oh-so-hip" SOMA Italian features "average" to "good" regional cuisine at "fair prices"; the "dark" setting with "body-shop decor" is populated by an "attractive Euro-crowd"; the "packed bar" and "good music" make this worth a roll of the dice.

Elite Cafe, The S M | 21 | 19 | 18 | $25 |

2049 Fillmore St. (bet. Pine & California Sts.), 415-346-8668

■ Pacific Heights Cajun-Creole serving "great blackened fish and blackened steak" to a "beautiful, white-bread crowd"; "try oyster shooters" at the "tiny raw bar" and the "good crab cakes", soft-shell crabs and "tasty gumbo" that satisfy almost anyone who wasn't born on the Bayou.

ELKA S M | 26 | 24 | 23 | $41 |

Miyako Hotel, 1611 Post St. (Laguna St.), 415-922-7788

■ "A mind-blowing dining experience" in a "beautifully designed" Japantown hotel restaurant; Elka Gilmore's "super-creative" Franco-Japanese seafood is a "tasty" mix of "lively flavors" and "gorgeous presentations"; despite "glacial service", most say this pricey "treasure of the sea" is swimming "among the best."

El Paseo Restaurant S M | 25 | 27 | 25 | $34 |

17 Throckmorton Ave. (Sunnyside), Mill Valley, 415-388-0741

◪ A stellar cellar – the "incredible", reasonably priced wine list and "romantic, old-world elegance" win kudos at this Marin "hideaway", serving "excellent" New French–Californian food; a few critics say "a fine kitchen in a rut", but all agree, it's a "great date place."

El Tapatio S — — — M

475 Francisco St. (bet. Powell & Mason Sts.), 415-981-3018
"Good margaritas and crab quesadilla" and the "best flowers in town" make this Wharf Mexican "bearable"; some complain there's "not enough food for the cost" and others warn "don't go out of your way for this."

Embarko S M 20 20 20 $25

100 Brannan St. (Embarcadero), 415-495-2120
"Fun, Eclectic dining" at this SOMA waterfront cafe features "pricey but good" garlic mashed potatoes and meat loaf and "coconut beer-batter shrimp"; other less-comforting dishes are a "little too nouvelle" for some, but most applaud the "witty but serious concept" and "great views of the bridge and promenade."

Emerald Garden Restaurant S M 26 20 24 $22

1550 California St. (bet. Polk & Larkin Sts.), 415-673-1155
"A little jewel", this tiny Van Ness/Polk Vietnamese charms diners with "extremely fresh food"; "flavors zing with cleanliness" in everyone's favorite "Vietnamese crêpes" and "Saigon pork chops that will bring you back"; "pleasant, considerate service" and the "lovely, little alley-garden setting" make it a "local favorite."

Emporio Armani Express Restaurant S M 23 24 21 $25

One Grant Ave. (O'Farrell St.), 415-677-9010
Haute cuisine meets high fashion at this sleek Downtown Northern Italian on the mezzanine of the Armani clothing store; for "good, quick lunches" in "chichi", "people-watching surroundings", try on the "special squid ink risotto", "solid pastas" or a "fairly priced" panini at the downstairs espresso bar.

Empress of China S M 19 20 17 $23

838 Grant Ave. (bet. Washington & Clay Sts.), 415-434-1345
"Plush Chinatown Chinese" that's still "good for classic banquets" and useful as an "introduction to traditional Chinese cuisine"; but many feel this empress no longer impresses ("a faded glory", "white-bread food") and has become a "tourist trap"; service is "pleasant if a bit stuffy."

Enrico's S M 20 18 18 $24

504 Broadway (Kearny St.), 415-982-6223
This classic North Beach Italian bohemian is trying to get on the road again after the passing of beloved owner Enrico Banducci; it has a "good jazzy atmosphere" and an "accomplished new chef" turning out "food that's a pleasant surprise", but the "bizarre view of boarded-up storefronts" and Broadway strip joints might explain why this historic, hip hangout "hasn't caught on with everyone."

ERIC Restaurant M 21 | 26 | 22 | $34

121 Spear St. (bet. Mission & Howard Sts.), 415-777-0330

"Very chic" SOMA New American that's an on-site "reincarnation of Etrusca" and its "beautiful decor"; the "creative food combinations" can be "inconsistent", but most find the dining "better than good" and the service "friendly", all of which makes surveyors wonder why one of "the prettiest rooms in the city" is "not more crowded?"

Eric's Chinese Restaurant S M 23 | 16 | 19 | $17

1500 Church St. (27th St.), 415-282-0919

Locals flock to this moderately priced, Noe Valley Chinese for "the best spicy eggplant" and "wonderful walnut prawns"; "the perfect neighborhood restaurant", it can be "crowded and noisy", which is why it's also frequently touted "for takeout."

Ernesto's S 20 | 11 | 19 | $18

2311 Clement St. (bet. 24th & 25th Aves.), 415-386-1446

The "robust food" at this "killer, basic Italian" in the Richmond area may be "swimming in sauce", but most regulars happily dive right into the "huge portions" of tortellini, linguini and lasagna; the "comfy, crowded" setting is "family friendly" as are the prices.

Ernie's Restaurant M 24 | 25 | 25 | $44

847 Montgomery St. (bet. Pacific & Jackson Sts.), 415-397-5969

The "best of the old elite restaurants," this Downtown French Classic draws "the Brooks Brothers crowd" with "gorgeous decor", "attentive" service and "much-improved" food; a few fault it for being "pricey" and "somewhat stuffy", but it remains popular for "true special occasions."

Esperpento S M 20 | 17 | 15 | $19

3295 22nd St. (Valencia St.), 415-282-8867

"Heaven" for lovers of tapas and paella, this low-cost, "funky" Mission District "hot spot" is popular for festive, Spanish-style grazing"; "the kitchen is slow", ditto the waiters and "better ventilation is badly needed", but "long lines to get in" are proof that it's well-liked.

Fana Ethiopian Resaurant S – | – | – | M

464 Eighth St. (bet. Broadway & Washington St.), Oakland, 510-271-0696

This Downtown Oakland Ethiopian offers a rare opportunity in the Bay Area to try an authentic African cuisine; "tuna with spices" draws special praise, but the overall menu is "good" and consistently "interesting" for newcomers to this change-of-pace ethnic.

Fat Apple's S M ⊄ 19 | 13 | 17 | $14
7525 Fairmount Ave. (Colusa St.), El Cerrito, 510-528-3433
1346 Martin Luther King Blvd. (Rose St.), Berkeley, 510-526-2260
■ "Out-of-this-world cheese puffs", "unbeatable oatmeal apple pancakes" and fresh berry pies "worth driving 50 miles for" explain the enormous popularity of these no-tablecloth, East Bay coffee shops, where diners also tuck away malts, fries and "the best burgers in the Bay Area"; note that if you're hungry the tab (and calories) can add up.

Faz M – | – | – | M
Crocker Galleria, 161 Sutter St. (Montgomery St.), 415-362-0404
At this new Downtown Mediterranean-Persian on the site of the former Circolo, chef-owner Faz Pourshoi returns to his roots with flavorful specialties like basmati rice with saffron, smoked fish plate and grilled scallops; the friendly, simple interior and welcoming staff enhance the evening.

Fior D'Italia S M 16 | 15 | 17 | $27
601 Union St. (Stockton St.), 415-986-1886
◪ Throwback North Beach Italian serving "passable pastas" and "sloppy sauces"; regulars call it "classic and comfortable", others say "food and service have declined" and "it's for members of the Tony Bennett fan club only."

Firefly S 24 | 18 | 21 | $26
4288 24th St. (Douglass St.), 415-821-7652
■ The "innovative" kitchen at this Noe/Castro Eclectic turns out "capricious multidirectional cuisine" that inspires comments like "it lights my fire"; despite "boring decor," many find it a "fantastic newcomer" where a "gracious, friendly staff" serves "creative food at reasonable prices"; no wonder it's "tough to get reservations."

Flea Street Cafe S 23 | 20 | 22 | $30
3607 Alameda de las Pulgas (Avy St.), Menlo Park, 415-854-1226
◪ "Charming" Peninsula Californian that's "an adventure in dining" thanks to a menu emphasizing "exotic vegetarian" dishes; some find it "too cutesy", but "beautiful service" and "constant innovation" make this "a treasure" for others.

FLEUR DE LYS RESTAURANT M 29 | 28 | 28 | $56
777 Sutter St. (bet. Taylor & Jones Sts.), 415-673-7779
■ "Flawless" Downtown Contemporary French "earns its stars (and top rating) day in and day out" with chef Hubert Keller's "exquisite, masterful cuisine"; prices are high, but it's "worth every penny to eat and be treated like royalty" in this "sublime", "romantic room"; vegetarian options, healthy dishes and a "stellar" wine list help this galaxy-classer "deliver on all expectations."

Flower Lounge S M | 23 | 16 | 16 | $23

1671 El Camino Real (Park Blvd.), Millbrae 415-588-9972
51 Millbrae Ave. (El Camino Blvd.), Millbrae 415-878-8108
5322 Geary Blvd. (17th Ave.), 415-668-8998

◪ "Frenetic" Peninsula and Richmond District trio offering "superb Hong Kong cuisine" with "authentic flavors and fresh seasonal ingredients", especially the "terrific dim sum" and "interesting seafood specialties"; the only knocks are "assembly-line decor" and matching robotic service.

Flying Saucer S | 26 | 17 | 16 | $34

1000 Guerrero St. (22nd St.), 415-641-9955

■ "Dr. Seuss becomes a chef" at this "wacky" Mission Eclectic where the "exuberant food" makes green eggs and ham look tame and "each plate is a palette" of "wild, architectural presentations"; reservations are essential at this "small", "crammed" UFO, and be prepared to share a table if fewer than four; but crowding and "snotty waiters" aside, most consider it "entertaining dining."

Fly Trap Restaurant M | 22 | 22 | 22 | $27

606 Folsom St. (2nd St.), 415-243-0580

■ "Good, unpretentious American food" in an historic SOMA building evokes that "good, old SF feeling"; try the "excellent Hangtown Fry", crab cakes, "wonderful creamed spinach" and "the best sweetbreads in town"; the "cozy environment" makes this a "choice walk-in place, especially on a rainy night."

Fog City Diner S M | 22 | 23 | 20 | $25

1300 Battery St. (bet. Greenwich & Lombard Sts.), 415-982-2000

◪ Innovative dishes of "good but pricey" diner food slide across the counter at this "glitzy" Downtown institution; the "small portions" of New American fare are "fine for groups who want to graze"; try the "great Cobb (salad) sandwich" on house-baked focaccia bread or the "world's best meat loaf"; critics call it "overrated" and "touristy" with "cameras going off everywhere", but most just smile and say "cheeseburger."

Fountain Court S M | 23 | 15 | 17 | 20

354 Clement St. (5th Ave.), 415-668-1100

■ "Consistently fresh, well-prepared food" at "reasonable prices" is the draw at this "pleasant" Richmond Chinese; standouts include "wonderful gingery won ton soup", "Shanghai potstickers" and "prawns with walnuts"; though many find the service "too casual" and the room "too bright", one reviewer insists "it's worth going here just for the caramelized eggplant."

Fournou's Ovens S M 25 | 26 | 24 | $42

Stanford Court Hotel, 905 California St. (Powell St.), 415-989-1910

■ This "sophisticated" Nob Hill New American may have lost a step but still provides "an exceptional hotel dining experience"; the "splendid kitchen" turns out "fabulous" lamb and other roasted meats, as well as "astonishing desserts"; "excellent service" and a "wonderful wine cellar" are further reasons why "you get what you pay for – and it's worth it."

FRENCH ROOM, THE S M 26 | 28 | 26 | $47

Four Seasons Clift Hotel, 495 Geary Blvd. (Taylor St.), 415-775-4700

■ "First class in every respect", this Nob Hill Cal-Continental exemplifies fine hotel dining; the "exquisite decor" has "old-style charm" and "service is always spectacular"; a few critics feel the "pretentious setting" and costly "small portions" are outdated, but the majority agrees it's an ideal "special- occasion place"; P.S."brunch is a three-hour food orgy."

FRINGALE M 27 | 21 | 23 | $31

570 Fourth St. (bet. Bryant & Brannan Sts.), 415-543-0573

◪ "French without the froufrou" are the bywords at this lively, top-rated SOMA bistro; Francophiles love it ("absolutely delightful Parisian") and claustrophobes don't ("too crowded" and "noisy"); but everyone enjoys the "fabulous braised meats", "crispy chicken" and Basque cake; with "charming service" and "lots of character", it's "all you hope a bistro will be" – "the only problem is getting in."

GARDEN COURT S M 19 | 29 | 20 | $35

Sheraton Palace Hotel, 2 New Montgomery (Market St.), 415-546-5010

■ Newly refurbished, this historic Downtown American Traditional is "absolutely gorgeous" and takes top decor honors in our *Survey*; "the most beautiful room anywhere" is "fabulous for brunch and afternoon tea", even if the service and food "can't quite match the splendor of the setting."

Garibaldi S M 22 | 20 | 22 | $27

347 Presidio Ave. (bet. Clay & Sacramento Sts.), 415-563-8841

■ A "lively neighborhood meeting place," this Pacific Heights Cal-Mediterranean offers "tasty, well-presented food": "outstanding" steaks and lamb, "nicely prepared fish"; it's "crowded and noisy", but "friendly service" and a "comfy setting" help make this a welcome "find."

Gate Five Restaurant S M 20 | 18 | 21 | $24

305 Harbor Dr. (Bridgeway Ave.), Sausalito, 415-331-5355

◪ This Marin American newcomer is "nothing fancy", but several surveyors say it's "better than the local reviews it received" and cite "good" seafood, "good" wines by the glass and "good" value; however, an "extremely short menu" does limit choices.

Gaylord Indian Restaurant S M 20 | 20 | 19 | $27

Ghirardelli Sq., 900 North Point (Beach & Larkin Sts.), 415-771-8822

1 Embarcadero Ctr. (bet. Sacramento & Battery Sts.) 415-397-7775

317 Stanford Shopping Ctr. (El Camino Real), Palo Alto, 415-326-8761

◪ Put Delhi in your belly at these elegant Indian cook-alikes serving "reliable Americanized food": the "curry dishes are splendid" and "tandoori chicken is delectable"; the Ghirardelli location has "great Far Eastern atmosphere" and "lots of smiles", but "high prices" prompt one to wonder "when did lentils and spices become so expensive?"

Gertie's Chesapeake Bay Cafe S M 19 | 17 | 20 | $25

1919 Addison St. (Martin Luther King Blvd.), Berkeley, 510-841-2722

◪ With a "faithful following" among East Bay theatergoers, this "hideaway" seafooder features Maryland crab cakes that "leave you wanting more"; a few find the rest of the menu inconsistent, but most declare it "shipshape."

Geva's M 22 | 19 | 18 | $24

482A Hayes St. (Octavia St.), 415-863-1220

◪ "Vibrant" Civic Center Caribbean offering "wonderfully exotic yet comforting food"; hot-and-spicy dishes aren't for everyone, but adventurous palates love the "mumbo gumbo and fritters", "best jambalaya" and "good goat curry" washed down with "just-like-in-Jamaica" homemade ginger beer; "service is slow as molasses," so go early if you don't want to be marooned while the curtain rises.

Ginger Island S M 21 | 21 | 21 | $25

1820 Fourth St. (Hearst St.), Berkeley, 510-644-0444

◪ Bruce Cost's new and trendy Southeast Asian–Eclectic on the site of the old Fourth Street Grill seems to be "struggling for an identity"; a menu that's "daring and delicious" to some is "too gimmicky" and "strange" to others; the early consensus is "good, not great", but even so expect "long lines" and high decibels.

Gira Polli S M | 22 | 13 | 19 | $17

659 Union St. (bet. Columbus & Powell Sts.), 415-434-4472
590 E. Blithdale Ave. (Camino Alto), Mill Valley, 415-383-6040

◪ These North Beach and Marin Italian siblings are ideal for a "quick chicken fix"; a few critics cry fowl at "upscale KFC", but the majority says "yummy" and agrees that the "wood-fire roast chicken is ethereal"; "difficult parking in North Beach" makes "takeout a good choice"; N.B. the early-bird special is a terrific bargain.

Golden Turtle S | 24 | 20 | 20 | $22

2211 Van Ness Ave. (bet. Valleto & Broadway), 415-441-4419
308 Fifth Ave. (bet. Geary & Clement Sts.), 415-221-5285

■ "Excellent gourmet Vietnamese" twins that win praise for "fresh, delicate", "inventive" food at low prices, including "superb sugar-cane shrimp", "very good crab" and what may be "the best first-course in town – vegetarian imperial rolls"; apart from "language problems" and a slow kitchen, these "cozy" places are as "good as golden."

Gordon Biersch Brewery S M | 17 | 17 | 15 | $21

640 Emerson St. (bet. Forest & Hamilton Sts.), 415-323-7723
33 E. San Fernando St. (First Ave.), San Jose, 408-294-6785
2 Harrison St. (Steuart St.), 415-243-8246

◪ "More for partying than dining", these pulsating Bay Area brewpubs appeal to "a lively, young Republican crowd" (over-30s should "sneak up the back stairs" to escape the brew-haha); "super" baby-back ribs, "fabulous" garlic fries and burgers raise spirits, but not nearly as much as the "great microbrew beer" and "meet-market" action.

Goro's Robato S M | 21 | 19 | 22 | $22

591 Redwood Hwy. (Seminary Dr.), Mill Valley, 415-381-8400

■ "Fresh, reliable" Marin Japanese with "very good sushi", albeit in "small" portions; "friendly owners" make dining here especially "enjoyable for families."

Gray Whale, The S M | ▽ 18 | 11 | 10 | $15

12781 Sir Francis Drake Blvd., Inverness, 415-669-1244

◪ A good stop after a walk on the beach or at Point Reyes, this Marin coffee shop/pizza joint has the best "cornmeal crust pizzas in Inverness", and a "good breakfast bakery" as well; it's "no great shakes" but nice to have around.

GREENS RESTAURANT S | 25 | 25 | 21 | $28

Fort Mason, Bldg. A (Marina Blvd.), 415-771-6222

■ "Nutritious" goes "delicious" at this renowned Marina Vegetarian with "outstanding" fresh ingredients, "unusual flavors" and a "top-notch wine list"; a few dissent over "oily food" and "self-important service", but most agree this restaurant with its "stunning waterfront view" is a "must-do for vegetarians" and for just about everyone else.

Grissini Trattoria & Wine Bar S M ▽ 16 | 17 | 15 | $24
Concord Hilton Hotel, 1970-A Diamond Blvd. (Willow Pass Rd.), Concord, 510-680-1700
◪ The setting is only a bit better than the fare at this Concord Northern Italian that serves "ok" but "nothing special" pasta and risotto; a variety of "reasonably priced wines by the glass" helps, but occasionally "inept" service doesn't.

Guaymas S M 21 | 24 | 19 | $24
5 Main St. (Tiburon Blvd.), Tiburon, 415-435-6300
■ "Splendid SF views" make this wildly popular Marin Mexican "unsurpassed for sitting on the deck on a sunny day"; as for the food, "they've got the formula down", meaning "refreshing Mexican" and "good margaritas."

Guernica Restaurant S M ▽ 25 | 20 | 22 | $26
2009 Bridgeway Ave. (Spring St.), Sausalito, 415-332-1512
■ "Call ahead for the paella" at this midpriced Marin Basque, where a "genial host", "large portions" and "delicious homemade bread" add up to a "local favorite."

Gulf Coast Grill & Bar S ▽ 16 | 12 | 17 | $26
736 Washington St. (8th St.), Oakland, 510-836-3663
◪ This Downtown Oakland seafooder has been in a state of flux with new owners, changing menus and shifting hours; the menu remains a question mark, yet a few faithful still find it "worth the difficult location" for a "good fish" dinner.

Hahn's Hibachi M ⌀ ▽ 21 | 5 | 11 | $10
1710 Polk St. (Clay St.), 415-776-1095 S
3318 Steiner St. (bet. Chestnut & Lombard Sts.), 415-931-6284
■ Van Ness/Polk Korean BBQ brothers that prompt diners to wonder, "how can they feed you so much for so little?"; for starters, they don't bother with decor or service; however, the "excellent chicken sandwich" and "spicy ribs" are always a good bet and make for "fabulous takeout."

Half Shell, The M 20 | 17 | 19 | $23
64 Rausch Alley (Folsom St.), 415-552-7677
■ Secluded, well-priced SOMA seafooder whose "dark, moody setting" is – depending on your mood – "serene", "romantic" or just "dull"; lobster is the Maine attraction, but there are also "great oysters and special bar deals"; the cocktail hour attracts a "convivial", "mixed crowd."

Hamburger Mary's ◐ S 16 | 16 | 13 | $14
1582 Folsom St. (12th St.), 415-626-1985
◪ "Don't forget your nose ring and tattoos" when venturing to this late-night SOMA institution where the Mary-makers go for "good but not great", "greasy burgers" served by grunge waiters; the "fringe crowd", "bizarre decor" and the "smell of risk" can be fun.

Harbor Village Restaurant S M 23 21 18 $24
4 Embarcadero Center (Clay St.), 415-398-8883
■ "Sparkling", "dressy dim sum" at a stylish Downtown Chinese where the Hong Kong–style cuisine can also be "excellent", especially "anything from the fish tanks"; the sometimes-at-sea service "has improved greatly", but you'll be better served if you "go with someone who speaks the language."

Hard Rock Cafe S M 14 20 15 $17
1699 Van Ness Ave. (Sacramento St.), 415-885-1699
◪ "The line for merchandise is longer than the one for food" at this "loud and commercial" Van Ness/Polk museum of rock 'n' roll memorabilia; affordable "big burgers" and "filling shakes" please tourists, teens and tween-agers, but most SF diners scoff "you've been in one, you've been in all."

Harris' Restaurant S M 25 23 23 $34
2100 Van Ness Ave. (Pacific Ave.), 415-673-1888
■ Superlative, Van Ness/Polk steakhouse that's "great for a martini-and-red-meat binge" in a "comfortable, clubby atmosphere"; there are a few beefs about "elitist service" and that "they à la carte you to death", but only a few.

Harry Denton's S M 17 20 18 $26
Harbor Court Hotel, 161 Steuart St. (bet. Howard & Mission Sts.), 415-882-1333
◪ "Well-heeled, over-40s singles scene" carrying on at a SOMA American bistro; though it offers "large portions" of "standard, competent dishes", "the bar action is the main attraction here"; "service has all the charm of a discount store", but K-Mart never partied like this.

Hayes Street Grill S M 25 19 22 $32
320 Hayes St. (Franklin St.), 415-863-5545
■ "Consistently good" Civic Center Californian seafooder with "impeccably fresh fish" prepared "to perfection"; other reasons it's often packed are "frites second to none" and "unbelievably good crème brûlée"; decor could use "spiffing up", but that doesn't keep away local politicos.

Heights, The S – – – M
3235 Sacramento St. (bet. Presidio & Lyon Sts.), 415-474-8890
Fiery young chef Charles Solomon (ex Geordy's) moves uptown to this refined, cloister-quiet Pacific Heights New French that replaces the bygone Le Castel; the clean, well-tailored decor freshens the once-stuffy interior, and polished service sets the tone for sophisticated dining on such dishes as seared salmon, spicy gulf shrimp and squab on a bed of polenta.

Helmand S M | 26 | 21 | 23 | $26
430 Broadway (bet. Montgomery & Kearny Sts.), 415-362-0641
■ Beloved, high-rated North Beach Afghan that cooks "intriguing" dishes full of "exciting", "stimulating flavors"; the "charming surroundings", "well-trained waiters" and "free parking" keep the hassle to a minimum; it's been discovered and prices are up a bit, but considering the quality it's "still a bargain."

Horizons S M | 14 | 23 | 15 | $22
558 Bridgeway Ave., Sausalito, 415-331-3232
◪ "Sailboats brush by your table" at this Marin Californian seafooder that offers the "best water views"; the food "has improved," but most still call it "mediocre" and advise, "have a drink – eat elsewhere."

House of Nanking S M | 25 | 3 | 9 | $13
919 Kearny St. (bet. Jackson St. & Pacific Ave.), 415-421-1429
◪ "Health code–threatening decor" and brusque service don't dissuade diners from this Chinatown shoebox or stop its food rating from going through the roof; some say it's "the best Chinese in SF" at bargain-basement prices that explain the long waits and cramped quarters.

House of Prime Rib S M | 24 | 19 | 22 | $29
1906 Van Ness Ave. (Washington St.), 415-885-4605
■ "Generous cuts" of "wonderful" prime rib and side dishes of "excellent potatoes and creamed spinach" plus a "turn-of-the-century SF feeling" win fans for this Van Ness/Polk beefhouse; "fast, efficient service" and "good values" add to its appeal.

Hunan Restaurant S M | 24 | 9 | 16 | $17
924 Sansome St. (Broadway), 415-956-7727
■ "Hot! Hot! Hot!" edge-of-Chinatown Chinese that's a real tearjerker; "fantastic" chicken salad, smoked pork, kung pao and other specialties make this "aircraft hangar setting" fly; "staff with personality" adds further spice to this "very affordable" scene.

Hyde Street Bistro S M | 23 | 18 | 21 | $28
1521 Hyde St. (bet. Jackson & Pacific Sts.), 415-441-7778
■ "Hideaway romantic" Russian Hill Italian-Austrian that's a "little cramped but cozy and cute"; "wonderful food" and "personal service" give this "European-style", "local favorite" citywide appeal; it's "hopping" and "needs crowd control", but "thank God it has valet parking."

Iberia S M 23 | 22 | 19 | $36

Ladera Country Shoppes, 190 Ladera Alpine Rd. (La Questa), 415-854-1746

■ "Something different for the Peninsula" – "superb Spanish food in a well-decorated setting"; the "great variety of authentic dishes" includes "rich, wonderful paella", "delicious oxtails" and "excellent orange cake"; it can be pricey and the "waiters occasionally take a siesta", but it's worth trying.

I Fratelli S M 21 | 18 | 18 | $22

1896 Hyde St. (Green St.), 415-474-8240

■ Popular Van Ness/Polk Italian where the food is *cosi cosi*, the atmosphere "cozy, cozy" and "reasonable prices" and "friendly waiters" keep things fraternal; those who find the pastas "mediocre" admit that "everyone seems to love this place."

Il Fornaio S M 23 | 24 | 20 | $27

1265 Battery St. (Greenwich St.), 415-986-0100
223 Corte Madera Town Center (Paradise Dr., off Hwy. 101), Corte Madera, 415-927-4400
Garden Court Hotel, 520 Cowper St. (University Ave.), Palo Alto, 408-853-3888
302 S. Market St. (San Carlos St.), San Jose, 408-271-3366

■ A well-oiled chain offering Contemporary Italian dining in "wonderful interior designs"; most surveyors laud the "dependable, satisfying fare" (try the roast chicken and eggplant pizza) and "fantastic breads", but "spotty service" can sometimes inhibit the merriment at these "trendy" hot spots.

Imperial Palace S M ▽ 22 | 20 | 19 | $27

919 Grant Ave. (bet. Jackson & Washington Sts.), 415-982-8889

◪ Upscale Chinatown Cantonese that turns out "costly but dependably well-done fare"; although "recent remodelling has made it less elegant and more noisy, Hong Kong–style", the "attentive service" is good for tourists and "great for banquets."

India House M 18 | 16 | 15 | $25

350 Jackson St. (bet. Sansome & Battery Sts.), 415-392-0744

◪ Downtown Indian with a dark, colonial atmosphere that's becoming "worn at the fringes"; while the "chicken tikka is divine" and "a taste of the vindaloo will send you to heaven", the kitchen can be inconsistent and turn out "careless, indifferent food"; almost everything here, including service, "feels a bit tired."

Indian Oven S M — 20 | 14 | 17 | $21

233 Fillmore St. (Haight St.), 415-626-1628

◪ "Creative Indian that works"; the rough Haight/Ashbury neighborhood may produce plenty of dharma bums, but "ignore the location and have a satisfying meal"; "uneven" service and non-Indian decor doesn't help, but it's always "a good value" here.

Iroha Restaurant S M — ▽ 17 | 13 | 14 | $14

1728 Buchanan St. (Sutter St.), 415-922-0321

◪ This Japantown Japanese noodle shop doesn't offer much variety, however it's an ok stop for a "quick bowl of udon" or "dependable ramen" at a "great price for the amount of food"; it won't win any awards for decor or service, but it's "convenient to Kabuki theaters."

Iron Horse, The S M — 17 | 16 | 19 | $24

19 Maiden Ln. (Kearny St.), 415-362-8133

◪ Downtown Northern Italian that's getting rusty, though some reviewers find its "standard fare of the 1960s" is still "better than expected"; its "dark" room is a "good old-boy hangout for lunch" with a "fine old-pro staff."

Island Cafe S — 22 | 19 | 20 | $21

Market Pl. Shopping Ctr., 59 Tamal Vista Blvd. (Lucky Dr.), Corte Madera, 415-924-6666

◪ Though the largely vegetarian menu sometimes "just misses", this Marin Californian in a "less than glamorous strip-mall location" is "better than it looks"; it offers "wholesome", "reliably fresh" food that's a "good value"; luncheon salads are standouts.

Isobune Sushi S M — 19 | 16 | 17 | $20

1737 Post St. (bet. Laguna & Webster Sts.), 415-563-1030

1451 Burlingame Ave., Burlingame, 415-344-8433

■ You pluck your sushi from little, floating boats at these Japantown/Burlingame Japanese siblings that offer "low prices" and "great fun for kids, if they eat raw fish"; some feel the concept has gone overboard: "a cute novelty but the sushi is not always fresh."

Ivy's S M — 22 | 19 | 21 | $28

398 Hayes St. (Gough St.), 415-626-3930

■ "Clean, well-lit" Civic Center New American that's a "likeable alternative to more popular spots in the area"; the menu may be "a bit all over the map", but "well-presented" dishes show an "innovative blend of textures and tastes"; "dependably good service", "relaxed atmosphere" and "pleasant decor" all win votes.

Izzy's Steak and Chophouse ◐ S M 23 | 19 | 20 | $28

3345 Steiner St. (bet. Lombard & Chestnut Sts.), 415-563-0487

■ "Fun, saloon-style atmosphere" prevails at this Marina-area standby; "first-rate" New York–cut sirloins and "super chops" are accompanied by "excellent creamed spinach and scalloped potatoes"; "good value", "friendly service" and a "nice neighborhood feel" complete the picture.

Jackson Fillmore Trattoria S M 21 | 13 | 17 | $25

2506 Fillmore St. (Jackson St.), 415-346-5288

■ Small Pacific Heights trattoria that has locals lining up for "hearty" Southern Italian fare, particularly the "incredible ravioli", "awesome sea bass" and veal chops; the "sterile setting" is "cramped and noisy" and the staff gives "too much attitude"; but there are no complaints "as long as they don't burn the garlic."

Jack's Restaurant M 18 | 15 | 17 | $30

615 Sacramento St. (Montgomery St.), 415-421-7355

◪ You get "a taste of the past" at this historic Downtown Continental bistro that, "like the Energizer Bunny, keeps going and going"; the "waiters are gruff unless you're known", but "wholesome food" and "good nostalgia" keep the "over-the-hill gang" happy.

Jade Villa S M 18 | 10 | 13 | $17

800 Broadway (8th St.), Oakland, 510-839-1688

■ Many Asian Americans frequent this "banquet hall–sized" Downtown Oakland Chinese, which fans say is "the place to get the hang of dim sum", although some of the fried items seem to "come from OPEC"; the crowds and noise can make it "like eating in a high-traffic intersection."

Jin Jiang Kee Joon S M – | – | – | M

433 Airport Blvd. (Anza St.), Burlingame, 415-348-1122

Peninsula Chinese that's "a very pleasant place to dine with reasonable food"; the interior "looks great" and there's a "nice view", yet one can't help but suspect that it may be on automatic pilot.

JoAnn's B Street Cafe S M 16 | 15 | 16 | $15

30 S. B St. (1st St.), San Mateo, 415-347-7000

■ This Peninsula American is "a cut above the regular coffee shop"; the kitschy decor is a "throwback to the '50s", and the "simple food" is "great for what it is": "tasty muffins", breakfast burritos and "excellent French toast" make this a "breakfast spot to keep on your list."

JoAnn's Cafe S M 23 | 10 | 17 | $13
1131 El Camino Real (Arroyo St.), South San Francisco, 415-872-2810
■ "Good road food" keep this Peninsula American (the older sister to JoAnn's B Street) "tops in its class"; "great breakfasts last all day" which is why it can be "tough to get in at lunch"; "pleasant service", "tight seating" and "retro" prices add to the classic diner atmosphere; N.B. the daily "specials" are just that.

Johnny Love's S M 14 | 15 | 13 | $22
1500 Broadway (Polk St.), 415-931-6053
◪ Watch out for "testosterone overload" at this trendy Van Ness/Polk pickup joint where a "beautiful crowd" convenes for the "great happy hour" and "late-night action" not the "passable food"; "big weekend cover charge" and "sexist scene" create a hate-Love's relationship for some; the new "Big Brad's BBQ" menu remains to be taste-tested.

Julie's Supper Club M 17 | 19 | 16 | $23
1123 Folsom St. (bet. 7th & 8th Sts.), 415-861-0707
◪ Self-consciously hip SOMA Californian supper club with "zany, *Jetsons* decor" that is best if "you go for drinks, skip the supper"; loud and crowded, it fixes "great martinis", "some good appetizers" and is "fun for large groups."

Julius' Castle S M 17 | 23 | 19 | $36
1541 Montgomery St. (Union St.), 415-362-3042
■ Perched near the top of Telegraph Hill, this long-lived, costly Continental offers "stunning views of the bay" and "decent food"; the "gorgeous location" attracts tourists, while "polished service" and "romantic ambiance" pull in locals with love in their eyes.

Kabuto Sushi S 26 | 11 | 19 | $28
5116 Geary Blvd. (15th Ave.), 415-752-5652
■ The "chefs put on a great show" at this "crowded" Richmond Japanese where the "dramatic sushi" is "the best in town"; "dingy decor could use a face-lift", but the beauty here is in the "exquisite", "impeccably fresh" raw fish; come with an appetite and sit at the sushi bar – you won't be disappointed.

Kansai M ▽ 18 | 15 | 18 | $24
325 Sacramento St. (bet. Front & Battery Sts.), 415-392-2648
■ "Pretty good Japanese for the Financial District", which means "consistent but not great cuisine"; "solid" sushi and tempura make this an "ok lunch spot", though "slow service" may make you late getting back to work.

Kelly's on Trinity M — 19 | 12 | 14 | $14

333 Bush St. (bet. Kearny & Montgomery Sts.), 415-362-4454

■ "Lively" cafeteria-style smorgasbord with a high ceiling and all-glass walls that's a Financial District "quick-lunch choice"; after figuring out the "confusing ordering scheme", serve yourself "inspired salads" and "gourmet sandwiches"; this Californian is also a "good bet for business catering" so put the number in your Rolodex.

Khan Toke Thai House S M — 24 | 26 | 21 | $22

5937 Geary Blvd. (bet. 23rd & 24th Aves.), 415-668-6654

■ "Always fun", high-rated Richmond Thai providing "small portions but huge, zesty flavors"; surrender your shoes, sit on the floor and receive "gracious service" of "deliciously spiced food"; "beautiful carved-wood decor" creates a "great ambiance" and it's "really good for groups."

Kim's M — ▽ 19 | 13 | 21 | $17

508 Presidio Ave. (bet. California & Pine Sts.), 415-923-1500

◪ Everyone loves Kim, they just "wish her food was more interesting" and consistent; still, this Pacific Heights Vietnamese-American offers a "pleasant atmosphere" and "affordable, quick meals"; "not a bad neighborhood choice", but not the best.

King Charcoal BBQ House ◐ S M — - | - | - | M

3741 Geary Blvd. (2nd Ave.), 415-387-9655

The relatively few surveyors who reported on this traditional Korean BBQ in the Richmond area advise that "nonsmoking" is not an option here: the "delicious BBQ" is "do-it-yourself", so "be prepared to be smoked" along with the food; it's "tasty" and affordable "if you don't include the cost of dry cleaning afterward."

King of China S M — ▽ 14 | 6 | 8 | $13

939 Clement St. (bet. 10th & 11th Aves.), 415-668-2618

◪ Imperially large Richmond Cantonese-Mandarin banquet hall that's only worth it if you're desperate for dim sum, since other dishes are "inconsistent" and "too greasy"; it's "busy and noisy" with "terrible service" that treats you more like court jester than king.

Kirala Restaurant S M — 25 | 13 | 18 | $21

2100 Ward St. (Shattuck Ave.), Berkeley, 510-549-2560

■ An East Bay Japanese with long lines for "the best sushi and udon in the Bay Area", "outstanding gyoza (potstickers)" and "excellent hibachi" fare; it's "not too expensive" for such "consistent quality" and "lively atmosphere", making it the kind of place SFers "wish would open in the City."

Kirin Restaurant S | 20 | 6 | 16 | $17

6135 Geary Blvd. (bet. 25th & 26th Aves.), 415-752-2412

■ "Unassuming" Richmond Mandarin Chinese serving "interesting, inexpensive food"; if the complimentary kimchi appetizer doesn't win you over, "the best sweet-and-sour soup" will; "Formica decor could use some polishing", but this is still a "local favorite."

Kiss M | 23 | 19 | 22 | $28

680 Eighth St. (Brannan St.), 415-552-8757

■ SOMA International-Eclectic newcomer popular with the design crowd who are tempted away from dieting by "colorful, beautifully presented food" and "extraordinary desserts" matched by sweet service; add "intimate", "low-key" ambiance and "casually elegant" setting and you know why everyone hopes this kiss will last.

Korea House ◐ S M | 21 | 12 | 16 | $23

1640 Post St. (Laguna St.), 415-563-1388

◪ Stoke your own fire at this "great place for a late-night Korean food orgy" in Japantown; "fun and tasty, do-it-yourself Korean BBQ" is a treat even given the "dark, dull" setting; it's memorable at least until the smoky smell of dinner wears off.

Kuleto's Italian Restaurant S M | 23 | 23 | 21 | $29

Villa Florence Hotel, 221 Powell St. (Geary Blvd.), 415-397-7720

◪ Popular Union Square Northern Italian with "satisfying", "tasty" fare: "appetizers might be better than entrees" which can be "inconsistent", but there's "excellent smoked salmon ravioli" and "smashing stuffed chicken"; the busy Pat K. designed the "fashionable" interior where you can "check out the cooks" in the open kitchen and the "attractive yuppies" "in action" at the "great-looking bar".

Kuleto's Trattoria S M | 21 | 21 | 20 | $27

1095 Rollins Rd. (Hwy. 101), Burlingame, 415-342-4922

◪ A "well-done addition" to the Peninsula dining scene, this "dark and smoky", "cookie-cutter" trattoria provides "predictable" but "tasty Italian classics"; the menu is "limited", but at least "you always know what you're getting."

Kyo-Ya Restaurant M | ▽ 25 | 23 | 24 | $38

Sheraton Palace Hotel, 2 New Montgomery St. (Jessie St.), 415-392-8600

◪ Expect "impeccable haute Japanese" with prices to match at this lovely Downtown room where special fish are "flown in daily" for "outstanding sushi"; some find the interior "cold" and the service not much warmer, but the majority say both "are beyond compare"; however, all agree that the "unagi is fabulous" and shame, shame if you don't "try the shabu-shabu."

La Bergerie S M 21 | 16 | 20 | $24
4221 Geary Blvd. (bet. 6th & 7th Aves.), 415-387-3573
■ It's "not fancy", but this charming Richmond French bistro presents a "good, complete dinner" that might be "the best bargain in town"; "large portions" (try the "great rack of lamb"), "old-fashioned" value and service have admirers cheering "thank heavens some things don't change."

La Cumbre S M ≠ 24 | 8 | 13 | $8
515 Valencia St. (16th St.), 415-863-8205
■ No-frills Mission Mexican that may be "the definitive taqueria"; "exemplary" roll-ups include log-sized "beef burritos" and "tasty lengua (tongue) tacos"; an "inspirational mural" watches over as you wolf down the low-priced goodies; the name means "the summit."

La Fiammetta Ristorante S 24 | 22 | 21 | $30
1701 Octavia St. (Bush St.), 415-474-5077
■ "Charming" Pacific Heights trattoria serving "good upscale Italian food" and "the best mushroom dishes in the area"; it's a "real sleeper", with an "intimate" setting that's "simple, elegant and special"; check out the tiramisu.

LA FOLIE M 28 | 24 | 26 | $50
2316 Polk St. (bet. Green & Union Sts.), 415-776-5577
■ There's *méthode* to the madness of chef Roland Passot at his beloved Van Ness/Polk New French; his "big-flavor" cooking is "stunningly presented" by a knowledgeable staff in an "intimate, informal setting" that's "less pretentious than other food temples"; this "dream come true" is "worth every penny" – especially the "bargain prix fixe."

Laghi S 22 | 15 | 21 | $28
1801 Clement St. (19th Ave.), 415-386-6266
■ "Top-notch" Northern Italian cooking in an unlikely-looking Richmond setting; squeeze into the "crowded room" and try the "delicious pastas", veal and "anything with truffles"; with "very friendly owners and staff", it draws only a few complaints for being "expensive for the avenues."

La Ginestra ◐ S ▽ 18 | 12 | 18 | $18
127 Throckmorton Ave. (Miller Ave.), Mill Valley, 415-388-0224
◪ "Great pizza" and "delicious gnocchi" are best bets at this Marin Southern Italian; while "underseasoned, canned tastes" are culinary sins for some, most are content with this family-run standby serving "ok" "family-style" food at "family-friendly" prices.

Lalime's S M | 26 | 22 | 25 | $31

1329 Gilman St. (Nielsen Ave.), Berkeley, 510-527-9838

■ Regulars at this "wonderful", "charming" Berkeley Mediterranean are mailed its prix fixe menus each month; despite "an occasional mishap", most of the "imaginative" dishes are "superb", "satisfying" and a "value" (especially the "special dinners"); devotees hope not too many people hear about this place.

La Mediterranee | 20 | 14 | 18 | $16

2210 Fillmore St. (bet. Clay & Sacramento), 415-921-2956 M
288 Noe St. (Market St.), 415-431-7210 S
2936 College Ave. (Ashby), Berkeley, 510-540-7773 M

■ "A panoply of Mediterranean tastes" and "a pleasant bohemian atmosphere" are easy to take at these Bay Area Middle Eastern mainstays; the "tables are close and you often have to share one" so be prepared to make new friends; "killer phyllo sandwiches", "great cheese karni" and "the best hummus around" at "low prices" help keep diners in amicable spirits.

L'Amie Donia M | – | – | – | M

530 Bryant St. (bet. Hamilton & University Sts.), Palo Alto, 415-323-7614

Chic chef Donia Bijan moves south from her Brasserie Savoy stint to this small, stylish Peninsula Contemporary French; in addition to the imaginative dinner menu, it's great for a light lunch and has fabulous buckwheat crêpes; the early word is that this charmer is a winner.

La Pergola S M | 22 | 18 | 20 | $27

2060 Chestnut St. (bet. Fillmore & Steiner Sts.), 415-563-4500

◪ "Quiet, consistent" Marina trattoria where the "rich" dishes are well-prepared but "not highly imaginative", prompting reviewers to debate whether this is "perfect Italian food" or "Italian without passion"; "somewhat steep prices" for "small portions" draw a few complaints, but there are none about the "friendly owners" who do a "good job on all levels."

La Petite Auberge S | 21 | 23 | 20 | $31

704 Fourth St. (Tamalpais Rd.), San Rafael, 415-456-5808

■ Perhaps this Marin Classic French–Continental was "better a few years ago" – or perhaps times have changed, making it seem "old-fashioned, though basically good"; a retractable sunroof makes it a pleasant summer destination for lunch or early dinner.

LARK CREEK INN, THE S M 27 | 27 | 25 | $37
234 Magnolia Ave. (Tamalpias Dr.), Larkspur, 415-924-7766
■ Surveyors love "classic" New American chef Brad Ogden's "rustic" Marin inn restaurant; the "beautiful, down-to-earth" decor provides a "comforting" setting for "robust" food that "raises American cooking to a new level"; this after-dark larkers' nest is also "a favorite for daytime dining", especially Sunday brunch.

La Scene Cafe & Bar S M 20 | 19 | 19 | $31
Warwick Regis Hotel, 490 Geary St. (Taylor St.), 415-292-6430
■ Despite the good food rating, this Downtown New American draws enthusiasm mainly over its martinis and location from the reviewers who comment on it; all agree that this scene is "very convenient to theaters", and that could prove to be enough.

La Taqueria S M 25 | 10 | 16 | $9
2889 Mission St. (25th St.), 415-285-7117
■ In the impassioned debate over which is the top taqueria in the Mission, this "funky" but "clean and friendly" candidate always rates high; all the basic requirements are met: "huge, tasty, cheap burritos", "great soft tacos", "delicious carnitas" and "fresh fruit drinks"; "ask for a crispy burrito – an insider's treat."

La Traviata S 23 | 23 | 22 | $25
2854 Mission St. (bet. 24th & 25th Sts.), 415-282-0500
■ Enjoy Rigoletto with your rigatoni at this charismatic Mission "jewel" where the "enthusiastic staff" serves Pavarotti-sized portions of "outstanding", "old-time Italian" food amidst operatic decor and "arias on the jukebox"; if you don't like divas and tenors, there's Verdi-little chance you'll like this, and even buffs sing the blues over the "bad neighborhood."

Le Central Bistro M 21 | 18 | 19 | $29
453 Bush St. (bet. Grant Ave. & Kearny St.), 415-391-2233
◪ Classic Downtown French bistro exuding that "old feeling" with "lively", "bustling atmosphere" and "traditional waiters" ("rude", "unless they know you"); the "good bifteck and frites", cassoulet in season and roast chicken are highlights of the "decent classic fare"; local politicos and celebs continue to make this "power-lunch" central.

Le Club S | 23 | 24 | 25 | $46

1250 Jones St. (Clay St.), 415-771-5400

◪ This tony Nob Hill French-Continental "turns back the clock" to when "intimate luxury" was taken seriously; "elders in the 'hood love" the "beautiful dining room" and "formal atmosphere", and a "talented new chef" might bring uniformity to the food comments, which range from "excellent" to "disappointing"; if only they'd turn back the clock on prices too.

Le Cyrano S | 21 | 17 | 21 | $24

4134 Geary Blvd. (bet. 5th & 6th Aves.), 415-387-1090

◪ "Real French food served by French people" makes this "affordable and elegant" Richmond locale a "pleasant" neighborhood "family choice"; some say "service can be rushed" and the atmosphere is "dated", but most agree that the "utterly reliable" cuisine is "timeless."

Left Bank ◐ S M | – | – | – | M

507 Magnolia St. (near Ward), Larkspur, 415-927-3331

Chef Roland Passot ventures to Marin with a bistro-ized version of his sublime La Folie cuisine; the bright, airy venue is an 1896 stone building where, whether at table in the dining room or on the sidewalk patio, you won't go wrong with the "turkey-sized" roast chicken or perfect steak frites; there's full-service till midnight, so bank on this moderate- priced comer as a good "after-everything" bet.

LE MARQUIS | 28 | 25 | 27 | $42

Plaza Shopping Ctr., 3524B Mt. Diablo Blvd. (bet. 1st St. & Oak Rd.), Lafayette, 510-284-4422

■ This Contemporary French "secret" in an East Bay shopping center surprises many with "top-quality" food without "cutesy flourishes"; a few surveyors say the "decor needs updating", but this "crowded but cozy" spot remains "outstanding" thanks to a "consistently good chef" whose high-caliber cooking is matched by "very personal service."

L'Entrecote de Paris S M | 19 | 17 | 18 | $29

2032 Union St. (bet. Buchanan & Webster Sts.), 415-931-5006

◪ French bistro offering throwback fare that's guaranteed to give you a "high-cholesterol fix" (the "featured steak frites" is served with a "homemade", "90-percent butter", "special sauce"); the "glass-enclosed room" is "great for watching locals parade", and despite "aloof service" it's still "pleasant for lunch or brunch."

Leticia's S M | 15 | 17 | 18 | $18

2247 Market St. (bet. Sanchez & Noe Sts.), 415-621-0441

■ They serve "hearty portions of dull Mexican food" at this "gaudy" Castro/Noe hangout, but the "friendly", "gay-but-so-what crowd" doesn't seem to mind; it's a "place to watch the boys", with "giant margaritas", "fast service" and "fun new decor" keeping this "incredibly noisy" meeting place incredibly "lively."

Le Trou Restaurant Francais | 22 | 18 | 20 | $31

1007 Guerrero St. (22nd St.), 415-550-8169

◪ "Quaint" Mission French that draws passionately mixed reviews: trou believers laud the "generous portions" of "simple, authentic preparations" (try the choucroute) and "terrific prix fixe value", while a vocal minority says it's "overrated", with "inconsistent food" and "disorganized service"; but most agree that the "charming" setting works for a "romantic evening."

Liberté ▽ 29 | 27 | 27 | $29

248 Sutter St. (bet. Grant & Kearny Sts.), 415-391-1555

■ Early word on this Downtown French bistro is *"mais oui"*; the cavelike, "see-it-to-believe-it" decor is paired with chef Elka Gilmore's exuberant entrees; both the "well-priced menu" and "stunning presentations" suggest a long, liberated life for Liberté.

Lichee Garden S M ▽ 21 | 14 | 15 | $15

1416 Powell St. (Broadway), 415-397-2290

■ "Huge tables of happy families" at this Chinatown Chinese prove that "great dim sum" and "large" portions of "authentically prepared dishes" at garden-variety prices keep everyone smiling; "check out the specials" which can be "astonishingly good."

Little City Antipasti Bar S M | 20 | 20 | 18 | $22

673 Union St. (Powell St.), 415-434-2900

■ North Beach Cal-Mediterranean that's "perfect for late-night cravings" as long as you stick to the appetizers ("baked Brie and roasted garlic is boss") and beware of "your eyes growing larger than your stomach"; the "out-of-control bar action" and location attract a "swinging crowd."

Little Henry's S M | 10 | 5 | 12 | $16

955 Larkin St. (Post St.), 415-776-1757 ⊟

339 Steiner St. (Columbus Ave.), 415-673-4407

◪ Chinese-owned Van Ness/Polk Italians serving "cheap and filling", "large portions" of "canned-tasting food" in seedy setings; some feel it's "good for the price", but a majority says "value doesn't mean anything if the food is bad"; Confucius says "never eat veal priced under $10."

Little Italy S M 21 | 14 | 18 | $23

4109 24th St. (bet. Diamond & Castro Sts.), 415-821-1515

"Homey" Castro/Noe Southern Italian that delights garlic lovers, even though the "good basic fare" is "solid but not thrilling"; "large portions" will fill you up after "a long wait to get in", but the no-reservation policy still has more foes than fans.

Little Joe's S M 15 | 9 | 15 | $18

523 Broadway (Columbus Ave.), 415-433-4343

"Basic Italian and lots of it" is served at this "diet-threatening" North Beach haven, where the "marginal, garlicky" fare is "cheap and plentiful", but the "scary bathrooms" and "filthy interior" are a big put-off.

L'Olivier M 24 | 24 | 24 | $33

465 Davis Ct. (Jackson St.), 415-981-7824

"Quietly elegant" Downtown French Classic serving "nicely presented food" in "a beautifully done room"; some find it "a bit pretentious" and all that "cream and butter perhaps outdated", but most agree this "lovely gem" is "too often overlooked"; indulgent gourmands recommend "heavenly hors d'oeuvres", "superb bouillabaisse" and "wonderful crème brûlée."

London Wine Bar, The M 14 | 15 | 18 | $19

415 Sansome St. (Sacramento St.), 415-788-4811

"More a wine stop than restaurant", this Downtown Californian offers an "excellent selection of wines by the glass" in a "friendly atmosphere"; "simple appetizers" are fine for nibbling between sips and regulars advise "always listen to Gary the bartender – he knows his wines."

Long Life Vegi House S M 19 | 7 | 13 | $11

2129 University Ave. (Shattuck Ave.), Berkeley, 510-845-6072

The Vegetarian cuisine at this Berkeley Chinese pleases most seekers of "good", "cheap eats"; some of the "mock-meat" dishes are disasters, but you get "big portions" of "surprisingly flavorful" veggie fare and it's served so fast you hardly notice there's "no decor."

LULUBIS/CAFE/RESTAURANT S M 24 | 22 | 20 | $30

816 Folsom St. (bet. 4th & 5th Sts.), 415-495-5775

"Super popular" SOMA Mediterranean featuring the tasty "boy-meets-grill" food of chef Reed Hearon; a "chic, young crowd" loves the family-style service of "heavenly flavored" dishes; the "cavernous but attractive" interior has a "joyous atmosphere", although some of the "staff have their noses as high" as the ceilings; N.B. reserve early, this lulu is hot.

MacArthur Park S M — 20 | 20 | 19 | $25
607 Front St. (Jackson St.), 415-398-5700
Popular Downtown grill that dishes out "blue-collar American food" to an "upscale" white-collar crowd; "finger-lickin' good" BBQ ribs and chicken and "amazing Cobb salad" draw praise and it's "worth going just for the onion strings"; complaints that this "yuppie hangout" is "too noisy" and "too '80s" are drowned out by a chorus that cheers "fun, alive and reliable."

Maharani India Restaurant S M — 22 | 21 | 21 | $26
1122 Post St. (bet. Van Ness & Polk Sts.), 415-775-1988
In a town still searching for great Indian food, this "blissful" Van Ness/Polk aristocrat is "always dependable"; specialties include "great breads" and a "heart-smart vegetarian menu"; "exotic decor" and "attentive" service will make you feel like a raja, and for a real passage to India reserve an alcove with cushions in the "fantasy room."

Mai's S M — ▽ 20 | 8 | 12 | $17
316 Clement St. (5th Ave.), 415-221-3046
There's "tasty and appealing food" at this Richmond Vietnamese, but decor and service are "missing"; still, "low prices" make it fine for a "good, light feast."

Mama's S — 17 | 13 | 13 | $18
Raphael Hotel, 398 Geary St. (Mason), 415-433-0113 M
1701 Stockton St. (Filbert St.), 415-362-6421
Mama's has twins – but too bad both her Downtown and North Beach Americans suffer from "lackluster food and decor" and high-for-what-they-are prices; however, "good omelets" and "tasty cinnamon French toast" still make for satisfying breakfasts; N.B. only the Downtown branch serves dinner.

Mama's Royal Cafe S M — 20 | 11 | 18 | $12
4012 Broadway (MacArthur Ave.), Oakland, 510-547-7600
Huevos rancheros and "homemade scones" get royal marks at this East Bay "breakfast mecca"; it's a madhouse when crowded ("like Bette's on acid"), but if you're at home with "funky decor" à la "the grunge look" and don't mind if you "can't find the waiter", pull up a chair.

Mamounia S M — 21 | 21 | 20 | $27
4411 Balboa St. (45th Ave.), 415-752-6566
"Bring a group" to best enjoy this attractive Richmond Moroccan where you sit on the floor and eat with your hands; the "savory menu" is loaded with "tasty", mostly meat dishes, and "attentive" Marrakech express service makes the "interesting experience" all the more pleasant; but for some surveyors, "once is enough."

Mandalay S M 22 | 12 | 18 | $19

4348 California St. (6th Ave.), 415-386-3895

The spicy, Burmese food at this "friendly" but "plain" Richmond "favorite" is a "welcome change" from other ethnic options; it's a "tasty bargain" with such dishes as lemon or curry chicken, Mandalay beef and "salads mixed at table"; some feel it's "too greasy", others complain of "long waits for the bill", but at least it's low when it arrives.

Mandarin, The S M 23 | 25 | 22 | $32

Ghirardelli Sq., 900 North Point St. (Polk St.), 415-673-8812

"Class-act" Chinese in Ghirardelli Square that's "back on top" after an ownership and chef change; "sensational tea-smoked duck", "terrific minced squab" and "especially good beggar's chicken" are well served in a "beautiful room" with a "superb bay view"; it's "a bit touristy" with high prices, but "great meals are once again possible here."

Mandarin House S M - | - | - | M

817 W. Francisco Blvd. (Anderson Dr.), San Rafael, 415-492-1638

Marin meets Mandarin at this attractive, cheery Northern Chinese that offers well-prepared, standard fare and attentive service; it's a safe bet and a "good spot for in-laws from the Midwest."

Manora's Thai Cuisine S M 24 | 15 | 19 | $19

1600 Folsom St. (12th St.), 415-861-6224

3226 Mission St. (Valencia Blvd.), 415-550-0856

"Crowded, bustling" Siamese twins "where you sense that the food is somehow just right" as in "delicious curries" that show the "proper balance of spices"; add a "cordial staff" and "traditional decor" and you can see why some call it "the best Thai the city has to offer."

Marin Joe's ◐ S M 20 | 13 | 20 | $22

1585 Casa Buena Dr. (Tamalpias Dr.), Corte Madera, 415-924-2081

This "straight out of the '50s" Marin Italian serving "good solid fare" family- style earns high marks for burgers and steaks; if you've eaten one too many Cal-Med meals, this can be a charming "old-fashioned way to spend an evening."

Mario's Bohemian Cigar Store Cafe ◐ S M 19 | 16 | 14 | $12

566 Columbus Ave. (Union St.), 415-362-0536

This "classic" North Beach Italian coffeehouse dishes out "the best roasted eggplant or meatball sandwiches" and "heaven in the form of focaccia"; nurse a cappuccino and chat up or check out the "smoking Eurotrash" and "funky, friendly" young locals – the eclectic atmosphere "makes you want to be a waiter just to hang out here."

Marnee Thai S M 26 13 19 $17

2225 Irving St. (bet. 23rd & 24th Aves.), 415-665-9500

■ Hole-in-the-wall Castro/Noe Valley Thai that enchants surveyors with "always awesome" food and a "psychic owner who will tell your fortune"; she might also advise you to order "great crab noodles", heaven-sent "fiery angel wings" and, for a "don't-miss dessert", the "sticky rice with coconut-cream mango"; "cheek-to-jowl" seating and "rushed service" almost break the spell.

Marrakech S M ▽ 21 22 20 $30

419 O'Farrell St. (bet. Jones & Taylor Sts.), 415-776-6717

■ This Downtown Moroccan charms diners with "good ethnic food and decor", a "very nice staff" and "great belly dancers"; eating with fingers from common bowls is "fun" to some, but "still seems weird" to others, and the high-end finger food doesn't come cheap, so "save up and treat yourself."

MASA'S 29 25 28 $65

648 Bush St. (Powell St.), 415-989-7154

■ "As good as it gets", this Downtown Contemporary French and "skillful, stylish" chef Julian Serrano are "Bay Area treasures"; "they go all out on presentation and service" to provide "an ultimate experience", and for these prices they should; what most praise as "uncluttered" design, a few criticize as "plain", "depressing decor"; but the ratings confirm: "still the champ" – "a national as well as local culinary mecca."

Maxfield's Bar & Grill S M ▽ 21 23 20 $32

Sheraton Palace Hotel, 2 New Montgomery St. (Market St.), 415-546-5020

■ Downtown Californian hotel grill with that "classy men's-club feel"; feast your eyes on the "impressive Maxfield Parrish artwork" and nibble on "reliable, tasty food" in a "fancy pub" setting; "great bartenders" help make it a "good place for power lunches", especially if someone else feels strong enough to pick up the hefty tab.

Max's Diner S M 17 16 16 $17

311 Third St. (Folsom St.), 415-546-0168

■ The "gigantic portions" at this popular SOMA all-American diner has one surveyor shrieking "oh my hips!"; put the diet on hold and go for the "good pastrami", "doughnut-sized onion rings" and "killer spicy chicken"; "retro decor" and "reasonable prices per pound" are great for family chow-downs.

Max's Opera Cafe S M | 18 | 17 | 17 | $19 |

601 Van Ness Ave. (Golden Gate St.), 415-771-7300
1250 Old Bayshore Blvd. (Broadway, off Hwy. 101), Burlingame, 415-342-6297

Operatic waiters deliver Wagnerian portions of "satisfying food" at this "boisterous" Civic Center deli; the singing won't remind you of Carnegie Hall, nor will the food match the Carnegie Deli, but go ahead and "enjoy" "great matzoh ball soup", "good corned beef and pastrami sandwiches" and "indulgent desserts"; similar classics hold sway at the Burlingame branch.

Maye's Oyster House S M | 14 | 12 | 15 | $22 |

1233 Polk St. (Bush St.), 415-474-7674

Ancient Van Ness/Polk seafooder/oyster bar that set the "SF standard for over 100 years"; new owners are "struggling to keep it afloat", but reports that "recent menus have slipped" aren't helping; "you either like it or don't": those who do enjoy its "good, old-fashioned" way with "reliable, fresh seafood", those who don't cite "grumpy service" and think it's "boring" and "out-of-date."

Mayflower S M | 22 | 12 | 16 | $20 |

6255 Geary Blvd. (29th Ave.), 415-387-8338

Richmond District Cantonese that's well worth the pilgrimage for "flawless dim sum"; this Flower Lounge spin-off has the same "noisy Hong Kong ambiance" and "cramped seating" as well as "fresh-tasting", "very nicely prepared" Chinese seafood.

McCormick & Kuleto's Seafood Restaurant S M | 21 | 26 | 20 | $30 |

Ghirardelli Sq., 900 North Point St. (bet. Beach & Larkin Sts.), 415-929-1730

"Class of the Wharf", this big, energetic seafooder boasts a "beautiful interior" with "great views of the Golden Gate"; the "menu is better than expected", notably a "first-rate selection of fresh oysters", "fabulous filet of sole" and "savory salmon"; "competent service" handily nets large groups and out-of-towners.

Mel's Drive-In S M | 12 | 16 | 14 | $13 |

2165 Lombard St. (bet. Fillmore & Steiner), 415-921-3039
3355 Geary St. (bet. Argello & Stanyan Sts.), 415-387-2244

These "campy", drive-in burger pits are "perfect for teenagers" but should be avoided by anyone who actually remembers the '50s; "greasy but ok burgers" and "tasty milk shakes" are good for a late-night fix – besides, "there's nothing better after 2 AM."

Mescolanza S M | 24 | 15 | 21 | $21 |

2221 Clement St. (bet. 23rd & 24th Aves.), 415-668-2221

■ "Unpretentious, cheerful" Richmond Northern Italian providing "big portions" of "always appetizing" food at "reasonable prices", including good thin-crust pizzas, pastas, "excellent veal" and "divine scampi"; it's "cramped and noisy", but the "friendly owners" blend lots of "warm feelings" into the mix.

Metropole Restaurant and Bar S | 20 | 23 | 21 | $32 |

2271 Shattuck Ave. (Bancroft Ave.), Berkeley, 510-848-3080

◪ It's "stereotypically French in all the bad senses" at this landmark Berkeley bistro; "classic game dishes" can still hit the mark, but many find much of the menu "passé", "heavy" and "overpriced", and service comes "with noses flown high"; lunch may be the best bet.

Mifune S M | 20 | 11 | 14 | $12 |

1737 Post St. (bet. Webster & Buchanan Sts.), 415-922-0337

■ "The sound of slurping echoes off the walls" at this Japantown shrine to Japanese noodles; there's "great soba and udon" and at these prices it's worth the wait; ignore the decor and do a bowl before the movies.

Milano Pizzeria ◐ S M ⊭ ▽ | 19 | 12 | 15 | $14 |

1330 Ninth Ave. (bet. Irving & Judah St.), 415-665-3773

■ Basic pizza joint in the Sunset that's a "neighborhood hangout" and "fine for families"; "fairly good" pies satisfy most tastes: "try the mushroom, onion and garlic combo"; eat there, take out or have it delivered.

Miss Pearl's Jam House S | 19 | 19 | 17 | $22 |

601 Eddy St. (bet. Polk & Larkin Sts.), 415-775-5267

◪ "Colorful and funky" Tenderloin Caribbean in an unlikely motel setting that reminds one reviewer of *"The Twilight Zone"*; submitted for your approval are "crazy cocktails", "great Jell-O shots", "flavorful jerk chicken" and "tasty yam fries"; this "hectic party scene" includes reggae by the pool.

Mom Is Cooking S M ⊭ | 20 | 7 | 13 | $14 |

1166 Geneva Ave. (Naples Ave.), 415-586-7000

◪ This much-hyped Mission Mexican hole-in-the-wall gets mixed reviews; fans cheer the "stunning mole" and other "authentic dishes", while critics contend "mom is getting a little tired" and cite "outrageously poor service"; bring cash: "they don't take plastic."

Moose's S M — 23 | 24 | 22 | $30

1652 Stockton St. (Washington Sq.), 415-989-7800

◪ "Bustling", multiwindowed North Beach brasserie that's the ultimate "in-spot" – a "people-watcher's paradise" that also delivers "refined, Mediterranean-inspired Californian cooking"; owner Ed Moose calls the shots at this "festive scene" where it seems as if "everyone knows everyone."

Morton's of Chicago S M — – | – | – | E

400 Post St. (Powell St.), 415-986-5830

Downtown steakhouse where they show you the meat before they cook it; the dark wood interior has a bit of a chain feel and though it's located downstairs, don't expect bargain-basement prices; the prime beef from Allen Brothers and the Stockyard has all the right credentials, as does this national operation.

Mo's Burgers S M — 23 | 10 | 14 | $12

1322 Grant St. (bet. Vallejo & Green Sts.), 415-788-3779

■ North Beach burgerteria that raises ground beef to new heights; expect "fresh ingredients and great toppings" at this "clean place" where the chef's ability to "cook meat exactly as requested" is impressive – it's rare to find something so well done, and that's no bull.

Mozarella di Bufala S M — 19 | 9 | 14 | $14

1529 Fillmore St. (bet. Geary & O'Farrell Sts.), 415-346-9888

◪ It's a "horrible location", but partisans insist the pizza has an "excellent crust, unusual toppings" and "real garlic"; however, buffaloed xenophobes say blame it on Rio, claiming "the Brazilian chefs" don't have the Italian touch; most would agree "it's best delivered to your door."

Nadine's S — ▽ 23 | 17 | 19 | $28

4228 Park Blvd. (Wellington), Oakland, 510-482-5303

◪ Laments for the now-closed "original" Nadine's in Berkeley indicate that this new Continental cafe in Oakland, despite good ratings, still has a way to go; it's "inconsistent but outstanding on a good day", though some say the food's "gone downhill" with "stale and limited selections"; the former Nadine's had a deserved solid reputation, so things may steady.

Nan Yang Restaurant S — 23 | 14 | 19 | $20

301 Eighth St. (Harrison St.), Oakland, 510-465-6924
6048 College Ave. (Claremont Ave.), Oakland, 510-655-3298

◪ The consensus on this Burmese duo seems to be that the Downtown Oakland original serves "better food", but the College Avenue offshoot is "prettier"; at either, "you have to know what to order" to end up with "bright, attractive presentations" of "well-flavored" fare (try the ginger salad and curried noodles) instead of "ordinary Burmese cooking."

Narai S | 24 | 16 | 21 | $21

2229 Clement St. (bet. 23rd & 24th Aves.), 415-751-6363

■ This "interesting Chinese-Thai" in a "lovely" Richmond setting serves "delicious, exquisite dishes" from both cuisines: try "great stuffed eggplant", "fabulous chicken satay" and "wonderful Hakka food"; service is "swift and friendly" and prices are low, especially for the quality.

Narsai's Cafe S M | 19 | 13 | 17 | $17

I.Magnin, lower level, 135 Stockton St. (Geary Blvd.), 415-362-2100

◪ Downtown Californian cafe located in a department store "where serious shoppers lunch" and try on "upscale soups and sandwiches" from the "limited menu"; the "miniscule portions" may not revive those who have shopped till they dropped, but most find it "very convenient", "good at what it does" and a "nice gourmet break."

New Joe's S M | 18 | 15 | 18 | $21

347 Geary Blvd. (Union Sq.), 415-989-6733

◪ Fans like the "good-sized portions" of "great pastas at reasonable prices" at this Downtown "SF traditional" Italian; but critics say this Joe's has "lost the touch", serving food that "tastes like cardboard"; most agree the service is "attentive" and the valet parking a "necessary bonus."

Nob Hill Restaurant S M | ▽ 20 | 19 | 23 | $32

Mark Hopkins Inter-Continental Hotel, 1 Nob Hill (Mason St.), 415-616-6944

◪ A Nob Hill fixture since the mid-'20s, this Continental is still a "pleasant hotel dining room" where "elegant service" hits the mark, as does the enjoyable dinner dancing; the "small, predictable menu" is no toe-tapper, but it's not a bad partner either.

North Beach Restaurant ◐ S M | 18 | 15 | 17 | $28

1512 Stockton St. (bet. Green & Union Sts.), 415-392-1700

◪ Throwback North Beach Italian serving "standout veal" and "above-average" pastas, though the rest of the menu rarely reaches beyond "fair"; critics find the "red-and-black decor" and "old formula" "touristy and tired", but others insist that "this old horse still has some kick."

North India Restaurant S M | 24 | 18 | 21 | $26

3131 Webster St. (Lombard St.), 415-931-1556

■ Union Street standby that is many surveyors' "favorite Indian restaurant in the city"; the "tasty food" is "hot when it should be hot" and includes "wonderful curries", laudable lamb dishes and "great nan bread"; the staff is "friendly" though a bit "pushy" and prices "high" but "worth it."

North Sea Village S M | 22 | 21 | 19 | $22 |

300 Turney St. (Bridgeway Ave.), Sausalito, 415-331-3300

◪ This Cantonese-Mandarin with a lovely view from the "great deck overlooking the bay" serves "the best (and only) dim sum in Marin", but the rest of the menu and the service are inconsistent.

Occidental Grill M | 22 | 19 | 20 | $25 |

453 Pine St. (bet. Montgomery & Kearny Sts.), 415-834-0484

■ "Definitely a man's place", this Downtown Eclectic lunch favorite has a "polished, professional feel" with "great martinis at the bar", where "cigar smoking is encouraged"; the "tasty though uninspired menu" includes lots of "rich, heavy food" served by a "sympathetic staff."

Ocean Restaurant S M | 22 | 6 | 14 | $17 |

726 Clement St. (bet. 8th & 9th Aves.), 415-668-8896

■ The kitchen policy at this Richmond Chinese seems to be "if it swims we cook it"; "you have to know how to order here" – regulars suggest the "addictive sizzling oyster" and "surprisingly tasty turtle"; low prices for "quality food" makes you forget the "bare-bones" decor.

O Chame M | 24 | 22 | 21 | $26 |

1830 Fourth St. (Hearst St.), Berkeley, 510-841-8783

■ In an area with a lot of culinary competition, this Berkeley entry should do well judging by its "beautifully prepared and presented" meld of Japanese and Californian cuisines, with box lunches highly recommended; this place "should be busier but not enough people know how good" it is.

Old Swiss House S M | 20 | 21 | 20 | $29 |

Pier 39 (Fisherman's Wharf), 415-434-0432

■ If you're fond of fondue, dip into this "touristy" Swiss chalet on the Wharf; the kitchen turns out "ample portions" of "straightforward" fare that's "not fancy but good" (try the "crisp and golden" rosti potatoes); the "location over the water" adds a view to an otherwise neutral setting, and regulars "love the fireplace on cold days."

Olive's Gourmet Pizza S M ⊄ | 23 | 14 | 17 | $18 |

3249 Scott St. (bet. Lombard & Chestnut Sts.), 415-567-4488

■ This Marina spot rates high in the pizza sweepstakes for its "wild combinations" (try the roast garlic and andouille sausage) atop a "very good cornmeal crust"; when "gourmet" is in the name, you can bet "prices are high", but the "innovative" pizza keeps fans coming.

Oliveto Cafe & Restaurant S M 22 | 21 | 20 | $30
5655 College Ave. (Shafter St.), Oakland, 510-547-5356
◪ Paul Bertolli (ex Chez Panisse) is now consulting chef for this Contemporary Italian with Mediterranean accents; though the kitchen turns out "consistently good" meals, critics call the cafe "overpriced" and "pretentious" with "lunch in the cafe downstairs far superior to upstairs"; the pizzas and tapas bar are strengths.

Omnivore Restaurant S M ▽ 22 | 17 | 22 | $25
3015 Shattuck Ave. (Emerson St.), Berkeley, 510-848-4346
■ This "Berkeley hideaway" aspires to be a homey, friendly Californian "neighborhood favorite", and succeeds; the "excellent" entrees are a "consistent treat" – for both herbivores and carnivores.

ONE MARKET RESTAURANT S M 23 | 22 | 21 | $35
1 Market St. (Steuart St.), 415-777-5577
◪ Brad Ogden's SOMA New American "upscale food factory" is just "too big and corporate" for some, who find the kitchen's efforts "disappointing" and "can't understand the raves"; however, loyal Ogdenites report "wonderful, zesty food" made from "freshest ingredients."

Original Joe's ◐ S M 19 | 14 | 18 | $20
144 Taylor St. (Turk St.), 415-775-4877
◪ This "SF classic" Downtown Italian may be "living off its reputation", but most surveyors agree the "great grilled steaks and chops" and "good pastas" still deliver, as does the "vintage decor", "efficient service" and "big portions at low prices"; original boosters wistfully ask "why can't it be somewhere else?", i.e. in a better neighborhood.

Original Old Clam House S M 15 | 11 | 14 | $18
299 Bayshore Blvd. (Oakdale St.), 415-826-4880
■ If you dig clams, head to this "down 'n' dirty" Mission locale; along with "wonderful clams", the hot crab sandwich is favored; otherwise it's "pretty standard seafood fare" served in "big portions"; at least the "out-of-the-way location" comes with "easy parking."

Oritalia S M 22 | 20 | 21 | $29
1915 Fillmore St. (bet. Bush & Pine Sts.), 415-346-1333
◪ "Japan meets Italy" at this Pacific Heights "charmer"; the "interesting concept" appeals to fans of "creative" fusion cuisine, although some view the combo as a "marriage that doesn't quite work"; however, the consensus says the "inspired, tasty food" is "great for grazing", but that "prices can add up."

Osome S M | 22 | 15 | 18 | $24

1923 Fillmore St. (bet. Bush & Pine Sts.), 415-346-2311
3145 Fillmore St. (bet. Greenwich & Filbert Sts.), 415-931-8898

Japanese bookends on Fillmore Street offering "solid sushi", especially the "great soft-shell crab" and "spicy tuna roll"; admirers are quick to use superlatives, but others soberly opine "sushi is sushi"; you can avoid the debate altogether here and "do the donburi."

Osteria M | 22 | 17 | 20 | $26

247 Hamilton Ave. (Ramona St.), Palo Alto, 415-328-5700
3277 Sacramento St. (Presidio St.), 415-771-5030

Trattoria siblings in North Beach and Palo Alto with that "genuine feel of a small Italian place", which means "crowded and noisy"; fortunately it also means "savory, traditional dishes" that are "great for garlic lovers" – try the "superior pastas" and "tasty pizzas"; sometimes "forgetful" service may make you think they focaccia.

Pacific S M | – | – | – | E

Pan Pacific Hotel, 500 Post St. (Mason St.), 415-929-2087

This polished, elegant Cal–Contemporary French shines in recently refurbished quarters in the Pan Pacific Hotel; chef Takayoshi Kawai (ex Masa's) has crafted a refined menu featuring sauteed lobster, crisp-skinned squab breast and filet mignon with enoki mushrooms; gracious service helps warm the marble-columned interior.

Pacific Cafe S M | 24 | 14 | 21 | $21

7000 Geary Blvd. (34th Ave.), 415-387-7091

Popular fish house in Richmond that nets praise for catch-of-the-day freshness at catch-it-yourself prices; the "first-rate seafood", "helpful service" and simple, "casual atmosphere" are all appreciated, and "free wine while you wait" helps bait the hook.

Pacific Heights Bar & Grill S M | 19 | 18 | 19 | $27

2001 Fillmore St. (Pine St.), 415-567-3337

A "neighborhood gathering spot", the PacBag is "clean and bright" with a "friendly", "low-key bar scene"; the raw bar with "the best selection of oysters" outperforms an otherwise "ho-hum menu", but many still tout the "good, reliable grilled fish"; the "relaxing interior" is especially welcome after the effort to find a parking place.

Pacific Tap & Grill S M | 17 | 17 | 14 | $20

812 Fourth St. (Lincoln St.), San Rafael, 415-457-9711

For "surprisingly tasty pub food" and "superior" micro-brewery beer, try this Marin brewpub; locals consider it "a great place to go" and enjoy the "outside dining area"; however, service is only "so-so" even by tavern standards.

Palio D'asti M | 23 | 24 | 22 | $30
640 Sacramento St. (Montgomery St.), 415-395-9800
■ "Cool, contemporary" Downtown Northern Italian that's moving up with a "young chef who cooks his heart out" preparing "amazing risotto" and "delicious Piedmontese specialties"; skeptics call it "seriously hyped", but most find the "sassy atmosphere" supported by "friendly", "accommodating service" "great for lunch or dinner."

Palomino S M | 20 | 23 | 20 | $28
345 Spear St. (bet. Folsom & Harrison Sts.), 415-512-7400
◪ New SOMA Mediterranean that's a "carbon copy of its successful Seattle flagship"; despite "gorgeous, bright decor", it still has that "chain-concept" feel: "looks like a resort" and has "formula-style cooking"; others predict "the kitchen will improve" and report that the risotto, crab cakes and salmon are "outstanding."

Panama Hotel S M | 18 | 21 | 19 | $22
Panama Hotel, 4 Bayview St. (B St.), San Rafael, 415-457-3993
◪ "The '60s live" at this "funky, delightful" Marin Eclectic-Californian, where wild tropical decor and dining "under the stars" are main attractions; some say "the food quality has declined", but "you can still get a good meal", and it scores "when they have live music."

Pane e Vino S M | 25 | 20 | 21 | $29
3011 Steiner St. (bet. Union & Filbert Sts.), 415-346-2111
■ Popular, "high-energy" Union Street trattoria whose "gutsy" Northern Italian food transports some – "I thought I was in Tuscany"; try the artichoke appetizer, pastas and striped bass; this "real Italian" "habitually doesn't honor reservations", but it remains habitually overcrowded.

Paragon S M | 18 | 15 | 15 | $22
3251 Scott St. (bet. Lombard & Chestnut Sts.), 415-922-2456
◪ A "meet market" with "good bar food", this throbbing Marina American is the perfect place for "sighting" "SF's best young talent" – "if you don't have a date, pick one up at the bar"; though it works well for the young and restless, others ask if this is "for real?"

PARK GRILL S M | 27 | 25 | 26 | $33
Park Hyatt Hotel, 333 Battery St. (Sansome), 415-392-1234
■ This tony Downtown Californian is a "great place to take a client to lunch"; impeccable service, "formal" atmosphere and "fine cooking" make this handsome hotel grill "a real sleeper"; "stiff" prices may be a wake-up call, but you'll "never have a bad meal."

Parma M | 22 | 17 | 22 | $24
3314 Steiner St. (Lombard St.), 415-567-0500
■ "Good neighborhood" Northern Italian that has "great Caesar salad", "friendly waiters" and moderate prices; simpatico ambiance makes this a "most un-Marina-like Marina restaurant."

Pat O'Shea's Mad Hatter S M | - | - | - | I
3848 Geary Blvd. (3rd Ave.), 415-752-3148
A raffish and boisterous sports bar in Richmond that features remarkably skillful Californian food at lunch but a dinner that's basically just beer and burgers; there's friendly service, a great beer menu, low prices and lots of big TVs.

Pauline's Pizza Pie | 23 | 11 | 16 | $17
260 Valencia St. (bet. 14th & Duboce Sts.), 415-552-2050
■ This popular Mission stopoff offers "great pizza in a bad neighborhood" at Pacific Heights prices; while the "Spago-esque" pies win raves, the "marginal" decor and location prompt some to "take out with the motor running."

Pauli's Cafe S M | 17 | 14 | 16 | $18
2500 Washington St. (Fillmore St.), 415-921-5159
■ "Nothing special, nothing awful" sums up this Pacific Heights American; it's a casual, locals-only spot with "a certain charm" that's best for brunch, but always a safe bet for "straightforward, hearty meals" at "the right price."

Pavilion Restaurant S M | - | - | - | E
Claremont Resort & Spa, Ashby & Domingo Aves., Oakland, 510-843-3000
Don't let the tony address of this East Bay Californian seafooder oversell you; the few surveyors reporting say the "view is great", the wine list is "good" and the "staff cheerful", but the food is "decidedly disappointing", especially considering the prices you pay.

Pazzia Caffe Pizzeria Rosticceria M | - | - | - | I
337 Third St. (bet. Folsom & Harrison Sts.), 415-512-1693
A simple storefront Italian near the SOMA Moscone Center that produces some of the best pasta in town; it's attractive and lively with friendly service, the lasagna is magnifico and prices are very modest.

Perry's ◐ S M | 17 | 17 | 18 | $19
1944 Union St. (Laguna St.), 415-922-9022
◪ Union Street dinosaur offering "great nostalgia" for some, "dank beer smell" for others; still a "late-night standby" with "good burgers and French onion soup", the once-active bar scene is now home to "over-the-hill jocks" – need more ice for that martini elbow?

Phnom Penh Cambodian Restaurant S M | 24 | 11 | 20 | $17

631 Larkin St. (Eddy St.), 415-775-5979

■ Van Ness/Polk Cambodian that's "a gem in the ghetto"; the decor could use some polishing, but "tasty, unique food" at "ridiculously low prices" more than makes up for it; come here for "an exotic change of pace."

Piazza D'Angelo S M | 21 | 23 | 21 | $24

22 Miller Ave. (Throckmorton Ave.), Mill Valley, 415-388-2000

◪ This "vibrant" Marin Italian offers "well-priced, well-prepared" food and attractively "remodelled" decor, but it can get "crowded" and "very, very noisy"; detractors find it "a little too trendy", "too rushed" and "too much like LA."

Pier 23 Cafe S | 15 | 16 | 14 | $20

Pier 23 (Embarcadero), 415-362-5125

■ On the waterfront, this American dive is a contender for Embarcadero's biggest "party scene"; there's "afternoon jazz" and the "outdoor patio is super"; despite some reports of "great cioppino" and "decent seafood", the "food is secondary" to the bar action.

PJ's Oyster Bed S M | 21 | 14 | 18 | $22

737 Irving St. (bet. 8th & 9th Aves.), 415-566-7775

■ There's "great seafood without pretense" and "giant fish on the walls" at this Sunset favorite; "heavenly fried oysters" and "the best 'chowdah' outside of New England" keep it "crowded and noisy"; the Cajun Festival running March through October is "not to be missed."

Plearn Thai Cuisine S M | 21 | 14 | 16 | $18

2050 University Ave. (Shattuck Ave.), Berkeley, 510-841-2148

◪ Popular East Bay Thai that serves "generally delicious" food at "a fair price"; a few complaints say "too sweet", "too hot" and "too American", but most surveyors still give this place raves and wait in line without complaint.

Plump Jack Cafe M | 24 | 23 | 23 | $33

3127 Fillmore St. (bet. Filbert & Greenwich Sts.), 415-563-4755

■ Named for Gordon Getty's opera and run by his son, this Union Street–area Mediterranean has fans singing its praises for "wild", "whimsical decor", "friendly but professional service", "best wine prices in town" and chef Arnold Rossman's "well-prepared menu"; in short, the word is out on this lots-to-love "winner."

POSTRIO S M 28 | 28 | 26 | $43

Prescott Hotel, 545 Post St. (Mason St.), 415-776-7825

■ Chef-restaurateur-entrepreneur Wolfgang Puck's good-as-gold-rush touch and the resident kitchen's "consistently great California fare" make this "stunning" Downtown eatery our SF surveyors' most popular dining choice; a few, who 'with a little bit of Puck' got a table, complain about the "deafening noise" and call it "too LA", which probably means "too many beautiful people"; N.B. double good news: original chefs Annie and David Gingrass have recently opened their own SOMA restaurant, and Postrio's new kitchen team maintains their high standards.

Prego ◐ S M 20 | 20 | 19 | $26

2000 Union St. (Buchanan St.), 415-563-3305

■ You can expect "dependable Italian" at this lively Union Street trattoria that "feels a little like a chain"; the food "doesn't aspire to greatness", but the servers apparently do – are they "sexy Italian waiters" or just "snooty" guys?; all in all, the "old favorite" is "still a lot of fun."

Primo Patio Cafe S M ⇏ – | – | – | M

214 Townsend St. (bet. 3rd & 4th Sts.), 415-957-1129

The few surveyors who report on this SOMA Caribbean say it's a "great bargain" with "the best jerk chicken in the area"; "friendly service and interesting food" prompt one committed Primo-tive to proclaim: "my unbelievable secret spot – please stay away."

Rasselas S M ▽ 16 | 10 | 16 | $24

2801 California St. (Divisadero St.), 415-567-5010

◪ The mood is "casual" and you "eat with your fingers" at this Pacific Heights Ethiopian where "warm service" and "great jazz" don't quite make up for "dark decor" and stews that are not to everyone's taste.

Regina's "Chi Chi Beignet" ◐ S 26 | 19 | 23 | $31

101 Cyril Magnin (bet. 5th & Ellis Sts.), 415-421-4254

■ They give a big taste of the Big Easy at this "tiny", "dark" Downtown Cajun with "fanciful" decor that's "romantic" to some, "puzzling" to others; all agree that the cuisine is "sublime", notably the chocolate bread pudding, pork loin, shrimp, crab and buttermilk biscuits.

Rendezvous du Monde M ⇏ ▽ 21 | 13 | 20 | $22

431 Bush St. (bet. Grant & Kearny Sts.), 415-392-3332

■ "Friendly", family-run Downtown Mediterranean with "great home-cooked food"; dungeon-chic decor is understandably "cramped"; all agree it's an "excellent bargain for a lunchtime rendezvous."

Restaurant Enoteca, The S M 22 | 18 | 21 | $30
933 San Pablo Ave. (bet. Marin & Solano Aves.), Albany, 510-524-4822
"A nice place to wine", this "authentic" Italian trattoria gets standing ovations for its "first-rate" cellar; but while most applaud the "rich flavors" of the food, chefs come and go so quality "varies"; the "quaint decor" feels "like a slice of Northern Italy."

Rice Table, The S 24 | 17 | 20 | $24
1617 Fourth St. (G St.), San Rafael, 415-456-1808
Marin Indonesian specializing in "tasty", "authentic rijstaffel" (rice table: many small dishes of food served with hot rice) that's on a par with "fine Indonesian restaurants in Amsterdam"; communal dining and "friendly service" make this ideal "for a party."

Ristorante Ecco M 24 | 24 | 23 | $30
101 South Park (bet. 2nd & 3rd Sts.), 415-495-3291
"Serene" Italian in a park setting that's praised for "terrific food": try the mushroom lasagna, linguine with pears and gorgonzola, and "terrific" smoked pheasant salad; add elegant surroundings and "solicitous staff" and you have a "tony hangout."

Ristorante Fabrizio S M 21 | 15 | 21 | $25
455 Magnolia Ave. (Cane St.), Larkspur, 415-924-3332
"Friendly atmosphere", "bargain" prices – especially at lunch – and "good risotto and pasta" are the draws at this Marin Northern Italian; a "disappointed" few say "overrated", but they're outnumbered by those who enjoy this "pleasant" "neighborhood find" where "large parties are handled with ease."

Ristorante Lucca S M 20 | 16 | 18 | $23
24 Sunnyside Ave. (Parkwood), Mill Valley, 415-388-4467
The "excellent Monday night lobster" is a good bet at this Marin Italian, but the regular menu is "standard fare"; "cozy, intimate rooms", "inviting fireplaces" and "friendly service" keep this a solid local choice.

Ristorante Milano S 25 | 18 | 22 | $27
1448 Pacific Ave. (bet. Hyde & Larkin Sts.), 415-673-2961
"Even the horrible parking can't keep away" enthusiastic regulars from this popular Russian Hill Northern Italian; "marvelous risotto", "fantastic tiramisu", "superb veal" and knockout gnocchi are reasons it's "always crowded"; add a "cute setting", "considerate service" and a no-reserving policy and you'll understand why you'd better go early.

RITZ-CARLTON DINING ROOM M — 28 | 28 | 28 | $51

Ritz-Carlton Hotel, 600 Stockton St. (California St.), 415-296-7465

■ One taste of chef Gary Danko's "superb everything" at this top-notch Nob Hill New American has surveyors announcing "perfection achieved"; when you consider the regal interior and "elegance-personified" service, then "every penny is well spent" for a "transcendental dining experience" that's "far removed from the hectic world"; a few world-weary critics "stifle a yawn", but for everyone else "this is the Ritz!"

Ritz-Carlton Terrace S M — 25 | 26 | 24 | $43

Ritz-Carlton Hotel, 600 Stockton St. (California St.), 415-296-7465

■ "What a setting for lunch outside" is the usual reaction to this "always charming" Nob Hill Californian; lunch might be a "superb salmon sandwich" and "spectacular dessert", and then there's "lovely afternoon tea" amidst the same "fabulous decor"; a few whine that "at these prices we should get the Dining Room", but they'd probably like Ritz towels and ashtrays too.

Rivoli Restaurant S M — 25 | 15 | 22 | $29

1539 Solano Ave. (Peralta), Berkeley, 510-526-2542

■ Even with "a few kinks to work out", "this new kid in town" is a "fast starter" with changing menus that offer "flavorful" and "appealing" selections of Contemporary American and Mediterranean cuisine; the "garden is lovely", but they ought to do something about the "substandard" decor and "horrible acoustics."

Roosevelt Tamale Parlor S ⇏ — 20 | 7 | 13 | $12

2817 24th St. (bet. Bryant & York Sts.), 415-550-9213

◪ For "the best handmade tamales in the Mission" try this "authentic Mexican hole-in-the-wall" standby that's dirt cheap but also "dirty"; the Teddy Roosevelt–theme decor loses voters, but the enchiladas and chimichangas win them back – again and again.

Rosmarino S — 23 | 22 | 24 | $30

3665 Sacramento St. (bet. Locust & Spruce Sts.), 415-931-7710

■ This Richmond Italian-French is "a neighborhood oasis" that's the best-kept secret since *The Crying Game* – there are no hidden sausages on the menu, just "great, creative bistro fare", "cute, artistic decor" and "friendly" "waiters who attend to every need."

Roti S M — 24 | 24 | 22 | $31

Hotel Griffon, 155 Steuart St. (bet. Howard & Mission Sts.), 415-495-6500

◪ Known for its "good roast chicken", "big booths" and "great ambiance", this Downtown Californian also gets some mixed reviews for "noise" and "indifferent service"; however, the "best french fries in town" and "great roast meats" are hard to resist, so most say "Roti gets my voti."

Rotunda Restaurant, The M — 18 | 22 | 20 | $24

Neiman Marcus, 150 Stockton St. (Geary St.), 415-362-4777

◪ Put down those shopping bags and grab a "great popover" at this Downtown New American; "charming waiters" and an "elegant interior" make it popular with upscale shoppers and "ladies who lunch"; however, "the decor is more delicious than the food."

Royal Thai S M — 23 | 18 | 20 | $21

610 Third St. (Irwin St.), San Rafael, 415-485-1074

■ There's "good reason" why this Marin Thai has "become an institution"; the atmosphere is "relaxing" and "friendly" and the fare is "consistently excellent."

Rubicon M — 24 | 18 | 20 | $41

558 Sacramento St. (bet. Sansome & Montgomery Sts.), 415-434-4100

◪ The "jury is still split" on this celebrity-owned (Robert DeNiro and friends) Downtown New French newcomer; most feel the "stark decor" doesn't do justice to "Traci des Jardin's inspired cooking", nor do some "spacey" waiters who are accused of DeNiro-like service – "you talkin' to me?"; but the overwhelming 'yea' verdict on the "superb" food shows that this Rubicon will be crossed.

Ruby's S M — 22 | 16 | 19 | $20

489 Third St. (Bryant St.), 415-541-0795

■ Head for the "zany red tomato sign" to get "great", "cornmeal-crust pizza"; physically, this "affordable" SOMA joint is "clean, well-lighted" and close to the Moscone Center, but not much else; however, it's also "fun and cozy" enough to make it "easy to be a regular"; Ruby's pizza is also available at Candlestick Park – go 'Niners!

Rue de Main — ▽ 23 | 23 | 22 | $32

22622 Main St. (bet. B & C Aves.), Hayward, 510-537-0812

◪ "Classic French without windows" is found at this "interesting" Hayward site that some find "disappointing" since it changed hands; others say it's still a "pleasant place" with "great" cuisine, "good" service and fair prices.

Sally's Cafe & Bakery S M 19 | 11 | 11 | $11

300 De Haro St. (16th St.), 415-626-6006

■ "Straightforward, dependable" and cheap, this "noisy" cafeteria-style Potrero Hill American cafe is "a great place to take breakfast and the morning paper"; later, there's a "primarily vegetarian, low-fat" menu and "terrific baked goods", which help regulars dally happily.

Sam's Anchor Cafe S M 14 | 21 | 16 | $18

27 Main St. (Tiburon Blvd.), Tiburon, 415-435-4527

◪ "Go for the view – only the view" and "eat somewhere else" is the caution on this popular "old Marin gin mill" and seafood house on the bay; the deck is "a great hangout on a sunny day", but beware of "kamikaze seagulls" who "steal your food – no great loss."

Sam's Grill & Seafood Restaurant M 20 | 17 | 18 | $27

374 Bush St. (bet. Kearny & Montgomery Sts.), 415-421-0594

◪ Clubby Downtown American seafooder where "crabby waiters" serve "delicious fish" ("broiled petrale is the dish" and "creamed spinach is mandatory"); it's an SF institution worth a visit for that "old-time feel", but get there early for dinner, the staff doesn't like to work late.

Samui Thai Cuisine S M ▽ 22 | 13 | 21 | $18

2414 Lombard St. (Scott St.), 415-563-4405

■ This Union Street Thai provides "consistently good", sometimes "unique dishes" and "bargain lunches"; it may be getting a bit worn, but the "bare feeling" is spruced up by "spectacular aquariums"; the consensus remains "a pleasant dining experience."

Sand Dollar S M 13 | 14 | 16 | $22

3458 Shoreline Hwy., Stinson Beach, 415-868-0434

◪ Some say this Marin beach-town seafooder is "reliable for a shopping-center restaurant", but most agree the food ranges from "average" to "ok if you like fish sticks", and service is "spotty"; at least it won't set you back too many sand dollars.

San Francisco BBQ S ⊄ 20 | 10 | 16 | $12

1328 18th St. (bet. Missouri & Texas Sts.), 415-431-8956

■ The draw at this "funky Potrero Hill haunt" is "tasty Thai BBQ"; the ribs, duck salad and sticky rice are features, but it's the grilled chicken with noodles that everyone flips over; "good, fast and cheap", there's "nothing better for the money."

Sanppo Restaurant S M ⊄ | 21 | 15 | 18 | $18 |

1702 Post St. (Buchanan St.), 415-346-3486

■ "Reliable Japantown restaurant" just about says it all for this affordable Japanese; it's "closet-sized" but "homey" with "efficient service"; the best of the basic Nippon fare are the tempura, eel and "fish specials."

Sante Fe Bar & Grill S M | 21 | 20 | 20 | $29 |

1310 University Ave. (Sacramento), Berkeley, 510-841-4740

◪ Depending on who you're talking to, this well-known Berkeley Cal-Southwestern is either "much better than in past years" or "not up to snuff"; the menu is "ambitious" and the food generally "good" if a touch "overrated"; something's bringing 'em in since the numbers and noise level are high – maybe the "top-notch bartenders."

Saul's Restaurant Deli S M | 16 | 9 | 14 | $14 |

1475 Shattuck Ave. (Vine St.), Berkeley, 510-848-3354

◪ "The Bronx meets Berkeley" at this deli that's "always crowded with ex–New Yorkers who insist it's not real NY"; mavens say it's "the only game in town" but "they should be ashamed of the egg cream recipe" and "small portions"; still, "you can nosh your kishkas out" on Reubens, pot roast, pickles and pastrami.

Savannah Grill S M | 21 | 21 | 21 | $26 |

55 Tamal Vista Blvd. (Madera Rd.), Corte Madera, 415-924-6774

◪ "Clubby-feeling" Marin Californian-Eclectic that "can be very good", but some feel is "erratic" unless you "stick to basics" like house-smoked and grilled ribs and chicken; it's always "noisy" and "crowded" so they must be doing most things right.

Schroeder's M | 14 | 16 | 16 | $22 |

240 Front St. (California St.), 415-421-4778

◪ It feels like "medieval Bavaria" at this Downtown German beerhall where "heavy, hearty veal and sausages" and the blue plate are the orders of the day; critics say this "greasy" "time machine" is "slipping fast."

Scoma's S M | 20 | 18 | 18 | $26 |

Pier 47, Fisherman's Wharf (Jones St.), 415-771-4383
588 Bridgeway (Princess St.), Sausalito, 415-332-9551

◪ These Fisherman's Wharf and Sausalito seafooders are "elegant in a touristy way"; bay views and "big portions" of good cioppino, fresh fish and fried calamari are the main events; it gets "crowded" and "can be noisy", especially when the sea lions start barking.

Scott's Seafood Grill & Bar S M | 17 | 9 | 15 | $13

2400 Lombard St. (Scott St.), 415-563-8988
3 Embarcadero Ctr. (bet. Drumm & Sacramento Sts.), 415-981-0622
2300 E. Bayshore Rd. (Embarcadero Rd.), Palo Alto, 415-856-1046

You'll get "dependable if unexciting" seafood in "upscale chain" settings at these Bay Area triplets; some promise "predictably enjoyable" dining, but others answer "not too often" – "ok for families and out-of-towners."

Sears Fine Foods S | 19 | 13 | 15 | $36

439 Powell St. (bet. Post & Sutter Sts.), 415-986-1160

Offering early risers "a rose of a breakfast in a thorny neighborhood", this 1940s-era Downtown diner has fans who line up for the "very best waffles with strawberries", Swedish pancakes and pies; but detractors complain about being "jostled", served a "greasy breakfast" and then "rushed by the waitress."

Seoul Garden Restaurant S M ▽ | 19 | 13 | 15 | $36

Japanese Cultural Ctr., 22 Peace Plaza (bet. Laguna & Webster Sts.), 415-563-7664

There's "capital" good food at this Japantown Korean; despite modest ratings and high prices, our few surveyors reporting enjoy its "quiet setting" and "friendly service"; the "chef's special feeds an army" and kids get a kick out of the barbecue cooked at the table.

SHERMAN HOUSE, THE S M | 27 | 28 | 27 | $52

The Sherman House, 2160 Green St. (bet. Webster & Fillmore Sts.), 415-563-3600

A well-known "special secret place", this high-rated Pacific Heights Contemporary French provides "the ultimate in pampered, intimate dining"; located in a small, "exclusive" hotel, the nine-table dining room "feels like a Merchant-Ivory movie set"; an "elegantly discreet" manner, "personalized menus" for all guests, "serious food" (a few say "too ambitious") and "perfect formal service" combine for "an outstanding experience."

Siam Cuisine S M | 21 | 13 | 18 | $19

1181 University Ave. (bet. Curtis St. & San Pablo Ave.), Berkeley, 510-548-3278

If you can "get past the orange plastic booths", you may enjoy "breathtaking Thai food" at this East Bay "favorite"; a few say it's "over the hill", but a new vegetarian menu could turn that around, and everyone likes the "good, friendly service."

Silks S M 27 27 26 $43

Mandarin Oriental Hotel, 222 Sansome St. (bet. Pine & California Sts.), 415-986-2020

■ This "classy" Downtown Cal-Asian provides an "excellent blend" of Pacific Rim cuisine – "sublime food" with "each taste a wonderful experience"; the luxurious interior and smooth-as-Silks service make you "feel like an emperor", and the prices make you wish you were one; with all that's "elegant", "artful" and "special" here, most wonder "why isn't it more popular?"

Sol y Luna M 19 21 18 $26

475 Sacramento St. (bet. Battery & Sansome Sts.), 415-296-8696

■ A "hip atmosphere" pervades this pulsating Downtown Spanish tapas bar which has "great salsa music for dancing"; the architecture is "sexy", and so is most of the crowd; some like the paellas, but most say "stick with the tapas and forget the rest."

South China Cafe S M ⌀ – – – I

4133 18th St. (Castro St.), 415-861-9323

Most everything is "basic" at this Castro Chinese; the exception seems to be "great potstickers" which, along with low prices, attract a steady clientele.

South Park Cafe M 24 22 21 $27

108 South Park (bet. 2nd & 3rd Sts.), 415-495-7275

■ Très hip SOMA French bistro with a "beautiful setting" "reminiscent of Paris – down to the classic cafe chairs and tightly packed tables"; the "limited" but "authentic" menu is "top-notch": try the saffron mussels, rabbit stew and lemon tart; it's lively, charming and fun – "a cute date place."

Spenger's Fish Grotto S M 11 11 12 $20

1919 Fourth St. (University Ave.), Berkeley, 510-845-7771

◪ "Bargains" in "old-style family dining" may still be had at this "noisy", crowded Berkeley seafood "institution", but most surveyors object to "being herded" and "long waits" for "frozen", "greasy", "microwaved" fish and advise "shop at the market, eat at home."

Spiedini S M 23 22 20 $30

101 Ygnacio Valley Rd. (Oakland Blvd.), Walnut Creek, 510-939-2100

◪ You get "consistently good Italian food" in a "comfortable, modern setting" at this "trendy" midpriced Walnut Creek spot; a few complain about its "formula yuppie", "small portions" and "nonfat, vegetarian dishes", but "great grilled meats" and "best pizzas" are the real favorites; everyone hates the noise.

Splendido's S M — 23 | 24 | 21 | $31

Embarcadero Ctr. #4 (bet. Drumm & Clay), 415-986-3222

■ Embarcadero retreat with a Pat Kuleto–designed "terrific rustic interior", serving "superb Californian-Mediterranean cuisine": the peppercorned tuna alone is "worth the trip for dinner"; a few say the heralded decor and food are "too studied", "ersatz", a "corporate concept"; but the majority reply – don't worry, be happy, this is "a splendido hideaway."

Spuntino S M — 18 | 14 | 12 | $18

524 Van Ness Ave. (bet. McAllister & Golden Gate Sts.), 415-861-7772

◪ This "useful refuge from the Civic Center jungle" can become "a zoo at theater time"; it's a "high-class Italian cafeteria" that manages to attract a stylish crowd and is popular for quick bites, especially the "great" pizza and pumpkin bread; though the food line is "disorganized", low prices compensate.

SQUARE ONE RESTAURANT S M — 26 | 22 | 25 | $38

190 Pacific Ave. (Front St.), 415-788-1110

◪ The bailiwick of celebrity chef Joyce Goldstein, this Downtown Mediterranean-Californian serves "delicious", "sometimes stunning creations"; it's "a tight ship" where the "staff is knowledgeable" and the "simple, healthy", "inventive food" is "always improving" and "also good for vegetarians and people on diets"; a few say this square has a rough edge: despite recent upgrades, stark decor remains "like a nice Denny's."

Stanford Park S M — ▽ 15 | 19 | 18 | $33

Stanford Park Hotel, 100 El Camino Real (Ravens Wood St.), Menlo Park, 415-322-1234

◪ Peninsula Californian in a "pretty hotel setting" that's "very pleasant" and "a good place to go when you're feeling down", but not when you're feeling hungry: the "erratic, uneven food" doesn't make it at these prices.

STARS S M — 27 | 26 | 24 | $40

150 Redwood Alley (Van Ness Ave.), 415-861-7827

■ "Still the best show in town", this "glamorous" Civic Center New American is trekked by a "high-energy, sophisticated crowd" who come "to gaze and be gazed at" and, oh yeah, the food is "consistently excellent"; while a few Klingons note that primo-star chef-founder Jeremiah Tower is not always around and insist everything here is "overrated", the loyal crew says "they treat you right even if you're not famous."

Stars Cafe S M | 24 | 19 | 21 | $26

500 Van Ness Ave. (McAllister St.), 415-861-4344

◪ Stars junior has moved to a spacious new Civic Center setting; there's the same "great, no-frills" New American cuisine, but what's gained in elbow room is lost in intimacy – "less cozy than the old cafe"; some disparage the "limited menu", but it's "a great deal compared to its parent."

Station House Cafe S M | 22 | 17 | 18 | $21

11180 State Rte. 1, Point Reyes Station, 415-663-1515

◪ "A refreshing oasis after hiking at Point Reyes", this "consistent" and easily affordable West Marin Cal-Eclectic is liked for breakfast and "fresh mussels and oysters"; BBQ'd oysters are a "specialty", and there's a "fabulous garden" for outdoor meals.

Stinking Rose, The S M | 14 | 15 | 15 | $21

325 Columbus Ave. (Broadway), 415-781-ROSE

◪ "Garlic for the sake of garlic" keeps this inexpensive but gimmicky North Beach Italian crowded with "noisy" "tourists who don't know better"; neon pastas and garlic ice cream raise the ire of foodies who cry "please, this is not Iowa"; critics say at least they got the name right.

Straits Cafe S M | 21 | 16 | 18 | $21

3300 Geary Blvd. (Parker St.), 415-668-1783

■ The "sinus-clearing" Singaporean cuisine in this "clean, quiet" Richmond setting is "delicious, fresh and a bargain"; there are "adventuresome choices" as well as "clever curries" and "superb satay" with "fantastic peanut sauce"; despite a few harsh words – "highly mediocre", "consistently uneven" and "greasy" – most reviewers enthuse over this "cultural experience."

Suppenkuche | 22 | 15 | 20 | $20

601 Hayes St. (Laguna St.), 415-252-9289

■ "It's like you're in the German countryside" at this "communal" Civic Center setting; the "refined" German fare is "surprisingly subtle and light", which is more than you can say for the "looming crosses on the walls"; the "friendly" owners and German waiters help warm up the "monastic decor"; most concur: "a real discovery."

Swan Oyster Depot M | 24 | 12 | 22 | $19

1517 Polk St. (bet. California & Sacramento Sts.), 415-673-1101

■ It "feels like family" at this no-tables Van Ness/Polk seafooder/oyster bar; chowder and Dungeness crab are first-rate, but many prefer to slide oysters at the top-rated raw bar; the "knowledgeable" "waiters are friendly guys", and no one would mind the "ugly-duckling decor", if only they'd "put in some comfortable stools at the counter."

Tadich Grill Ⓜ | 22 | 19 | 19 | $26
240 California St. (bet. Battery & Front Sts.), 415-391-1849
◪ "Classic" Downtown seafooder that can be counted on for "always wonderful fish": try "great broiled petrale", "fabulous poached salmon" and "the best cioppino in town"; perfect for a "clubby lunch", some find the "cooking style is a step back in time", but loyalists declare "it's nice to know some things never change", especially the Jurassic-period waiters.

Taiwan Restaurant ◐ Ⓢ Ⓜ | 16 | 7 | 10 | $16
2071 University Ave. (Shattuck Ave.), Berkeley, 510-845-1456
◪ While this "authentic" Berkeley Taiwanese is known for "great noodle dishes and steamed buns", some object to "dirty" conditions and sloppy preparations – but "if it's 1 or 2 AM and you're starving, go for it."

Tanuki Ⓢ Ⓜ | ▽ 23 | 14 | 21 | $21
4419 California St. (6th Ave.), 415-752-5740
■ "Friendly service", "decent dinners" and "good sushi" prevail at this "funky" but "cute" Richmond Japanese, where soft-shell-crab sushi is a specialty; "portions are large", prices are "low" and everything here is "well done", except, of course, the raw fish.

Taqueria Mission Ⓢ Ⓜ ⊄ | ▽ 22 | 7 | 11 | $9
4798 Mission St. (Omomdaja St.), 415-469-5053
■ This long-running Mission Mexican is "burrito heaven"; at these prices don't expect decor or service, but it's "clean and organized" and the "tasty tacos" and "fabulous fruit drinks" always fit the bill.

Tarantino's Restaurant Ⓢ Ⓜ | – | – | – | M
206 Jefferson St. (Taylor St.), 415-775-5600
Touristy Wharf Italian that may be on the rebound; the small number who surveyed this "old standby" rated it up in every category; skeptics ask "do you really need to go to the Wharf for Italian?", but those who did say "not bad for lunch, and a great view of the sea lions."

Thep Phanom Ⓢ Ⓜ | 26 | 15 | 20 | $20
400 Waller St. (Fillmore St.), 415-431-2526
◪ This terrific Haight-Ashbury Thai gets honors for "finest in SF"; the word is out and crowds willingly venture to this unprepossessing storefront in a "scary" neighborhood for "unsurpassed food" that is "clean and elegantly prepared" (try the shredded salads, coconut-chicken soup, curries and "best crêpes in town"); "even if you can't say the name, you'll never forget this place."

Thornhill Cafe S M | 23 | 18 | 22 | $27

5761 Thornhill Dr. (Grisborne St.), Oakland, 510-339-0646

■ "A gem in Oakland Hills", this "continually improving" Eclectic-French-Thai has an "innovative, lively menu" including "superb duck"; "enjoy the patio for lunch" at this "well-kept secret" that "deserves return visits."

Ti Bacio Ristorante S M | 18 | 16 | 19 | $24

5912 College Ave. (bet. Chabot & Claremont Aves.), Oakland, 510-428-1703

◪ While some hail the "satisfying light food" at this East Bay Italian, others say the "lean cuisine" "is good to your heart but a bit dull to the tongue"; the new location is "pretty", but former amours feel it's "gone downhill since moving", leading some to kiss this place good-bye.

Ti Couz S M | 23 | 17 | 17 | $15

3108 16th St. (bet. Valencia & Guerrero Sts.), 415-252-7373

■ "Zany" Mission French with "a wide variety" of Brittany-style, buckwheat crêpes; even "slow", "hipper-than-thou service" and "cattle-car" conditions can't squelch enthusiasm for its "very affordable" dinner and dessert crêpes, "even better onion soup" and "monster salads."

Tommaso's Restaurant S | 22 | 15 | 17 | $20

1042 Kearny St. (bet. Pacific & Broadway), 415-398-9696

■ Brick-oven pizza is the star at this North Beach Southern Italian, with important supporting roles for "super calzone" and "tasty lasagna" – and don't be surprised to find director Francis Ford Coppola tucking into them; "crowded and fun", it's "a worthy institution" and "good for families."

Tommy's Joynt ◐ S M ⌿ | 12 | 13 | 10 | $13

1101 Geary Blvd. (Van Ness Ave.), 415-775-4216

◪ Long-running Van Ness/Polk Hofbrau that's "good for late-night grease" as long as you wash it down with lotsa beer; "the food is left on the steam tables too long" and even "the signature buffalo stew is overrated", but it's "ok for a cheap fill-up" – just don't expect them to check the oil; the setting is "smoky, dark" and filled with shady characters.

Tommy Toy's Chinoise S M | 25 | 26 | 24 | $40

655 Montgomery St. (Washington St.), 415-397-4888

■ Haute Chinoise wins raves at this "elegant, finely honed" Downtowner where the beautifully presented, "creative cuisine" shows a French influence; the "lovely antique-adorned interior" and "tag team of waiters" "make you feel like royalty"; the "bargain" lunch is "half the price of dinner", which "would be better on an expense account."

Ton Kiang Restaurant [S] [M] 24 | 13 | 19 | $19

3148 Geary Blvd. (Spruce St.), 415-752-4440
5821 Geary Blvd. (22nd Ave.), 415-387-8273

■ It's "Hakka heaven" (Northern Chinese) at these popular Richmond siblings, where there's "consistently good" dim sum, and the extensive, multiregional menu includes "fabulous claypot dishes" and "excellent seafood"; prices have risen since a remodelling (probably too recent to affect ratings), but the "consistently delicious food" is definitely still worth it.

Tortola Restaurant [S] 19 | 16 | 17 | $18

3640 Sacramento St. (bet. Spruce & Locust Sts.), 415-929-8181
Stonestown Galleria, 3251 20th Ave. (bet. Buckingham & Holloway Aves.), 415-566-4336 [M] ⊄
Crocker Galleria, 50 Post St. (Sutter), 415-986-8678 [M] ⊄

■ "Safely spicy" cooking and "upbeat" atmosphere make these Mexican-Southwestern clones "great for families with kids"; all ages go for the "signature" chicken tamales, SW pizza and Caesar salad with "to-cry-for polenta croutons"; it's a formula, but it's "healthy", "reliable, affordable" and "fast."

Tourelle Cafe [S] [M] 22 | 27 | 23 | $32

3565 Mt. Diablo Blvd. (bet. Oak Hill & Happy Valley Rds.), Lafayette, 510-284-3565

◪ The "beautiful setting" and lofty reputation are still superior to the menu at this "charming" East Bay French, where the food is "good" but "ought to be great"; everyone hopes the new ownership will help this restaurant reach its potential; service is already "much improved", and it's "lovely for brunch."

Trattoria Contadina [S] [M] 19 | 14 | 17 | $24

1800 Mason St. (Union St.), 415-982-5728

◪ What the "reliable home-cooked food" at this popular North Beach Italian lacks in quality, it makes up for in quantity; "huge portions" of "hearty" pastas plus "friendly service" and "homey atmosphere" add up to a "good, cheap family-style spot."

Tre Fratelli [S] [M] 19 | 17 | 18 | $23

2101 Sutter St. (Steiner St.), 415-931-0701

◪ Mixed reviews go to this Pacific Heights Italian: fans love the "large servings" of "hearty, garlicky dishes", but dissenters find the "limp", "oily pastas" not worth the "long waits for tables"; cucina aside, it's "a good midweek hangout after work."

Trio Cafe S ⊄ | 20 | 15 | 18 | $13 |

1870 Fillmore St. (bet. Bush & Sutter Sts.), 415-563-2248

■ The "morning paper and breakfast" crowd love to "dive into a bowl of caffè latte" and nibble a scone at this Pacific Heights coffeehouse; later, "tasty sandwiches" and "pre-prepared but good mini-pizzas" are "great for a quick snack or light lunch"; no one seems to mind the nondecor or slow but "family-friendly" service.

Tu Lan M ⊄ | 24 | 2 | 10 | $11 |

8 Sixth St. (Market St.), 415-626-0927

■ There's "amazingly good food at amazingly low prices" at this Downtown Vietnamese storefront where the food rating rises as the "dumpy decor" rating drops; however, the "dicey neighborhood" is the "worst location possible", so all but the adventuresome advise "park as close as possible", take out and get out.

231 Ellsworth M | 27 | 23 | 25 | $40 |

231 S. Ellsworth St. (3rd Ave.), San Mateo, 415-347-7231

■ "The best French in the 'burbs" may be at this "casual, stylish" Peninsula contemporary "gem"; the refined cooking is "exquisitely presented" with "quietly high-level service"; wild-mushroom dishes and desserts get raves; for some, "the lost-in-time, pink-and-beige decor" and "stiff prices" detract, but at lunch and dinner the prix fixe "is a deal."

Umberto's Restaurant M | 20 | 21 | 18 | $30 |

141 Steuart St. (bet. Mission & Howard Sts.), 415-543-8021

■ Patrizio Sacchetto (ex Blue Fox) has replaced "Chef Boyardee" and turned this "subterranean" SOMA Northern Italian into a "gourmet house"; somewhat "uppity" service aside, its "romantic, cavelike atmosphere" and "much-improved menu" make it "a rising star."

U.S. Restaurant ⊄ | 13 | 7 | 14 | $15 |

431 Columbus Ave. (Green St.), 415-362-6251

◪ "If you're craving short-order cafe food" drop in at this "here-since-1900" North Beach American-Italian; "basic grub" in "large portions" includes a "good" steak sandwich, ravioli, "mama's meat loaf" and the "fried calamari Friday special", all at "bargain prices"; the unimpressed, non-nostalgic respond "the Salvation Army is better, and free."

Vanessi's Nob Hill S M | 19 | 18 | 19 | $30 |

1177 California St. (Jones St.), 415-771-2422

◪ Some who "remember the old days in North Beach" say this transplanted Nob Hill Italian "seems to be slipping"; but supporters insist that it still has "great Caesar salads" at lunch and "friendly service"; insiders advise "sit at the counter" and "stick to pasta and chicken."

Venezia S M — 21 | 21 | 20 | $22

1799 University Ave. (Grant St.), Berkeley, 510-849-4681

"Good value" and "reliable Italian food" meet at this novel East Bay trattoria; "you have to love the old-world look", complete with fountain, mural and clothesline ("makes me want to hang out the laundry and play bocce with my grandfather"), and most do, calling it a "delightful", "pleasant", "family-oriented" addition to the neighborhood.

Venticello Ristorante S M — 20 | 20 | 18 | $32

1257 Taylor St. (Washington St.), 415-922-2545

"Intimate, romantic" Nob Hill Northern Italian that draws praise for its "great veal chop" and "fantastic polenta with portobellos", but also gets complaints for food that "lacks passion" and a staff that turns the cold shoulder; this "always busy" eatery seems to play "chef of the week" and quality varies accordingly.

Vicolo Pizzeria S M — 25 | 13 | 13 | $16

201 Ivy St. (Franklin St.), 415-863-2382

473 University Ave. (Kipling St.), Palo Alto, 415-324-4877

Be warned, these top-rated Civic Center and Palo Alto pizzerias "can be addictive" – all it takes is a taste of the "terrific cornmeal crust" with "fresh, gourmet toppings"; they're "cute and trendy" despite lack of service and decor, and well worth the price per slice.

Vic Stewart's S M — 23 | 26 | 22 | $34

850 S. Broadway (Newell St.), Walnut Creek, 510-943-5666

"You'll be riding in style" at this Walnut Creek beefery, where "succulent steaks" are served in "cozy, highly romantic, private Pullman dining cars"; add a "great bar and wine list" and "beautiful surroundings with good parking" and this "excellent but pricey" newcomer is right on track.

Victor's Restaurant S M — 23 | 26 | 22 | $37

Westin St. Francis Hotel, 335 Powell St. (bet. Post & Geary Sts.), 415-744-0253

High on the 32nd floor, the "doting staff" at this Downtown New French– Californian serves "fine food" that actually matches the "breathtaking views"; and the stylish setting also makes it "great for Sunday brunch"; lovebirds take note: "this is the place to propose."

Vince S.F. ◐ S — 16 | 15 | 16 | $21

395 Hayes St. (Gough St.), 415-864-4824

"Trendy" Civic Center Italian attracts "a pretentious young crowd" that doesn't seem to notice "food that falls flat" and "amateurish service"; the "small portions" are at least "cheap and quick for pre-arts", and "dishes to share" satisfy some, but "stark decor" and "laid-back ambiance" can make it feel "like eating in space – no atmosphere."

Vivande Porta Via S M 25 | 17 | 19 | $26
2125 Fillmore St. (bet. California & Sacramento Sts.), 415-346-4430
■ "The foodies' choice for lunch", this "pricey" Pacific Heights Italian deli offers "tasty eat-here or take-out treats"; chef Carlo Middione puts on a show, preparing "passionate", "quintessential Southern Italian" dishes; now open for dinner, but many agree that with "cramped seating" it's still "best for lunch."

¡Wa-Ha-Ka! Oaxaca Mexican Grill S M 17 | 13 | 13 | $11
1489 Folsom St. (11th St.), 415-861-1410
2141 Polk St. (Broadway), 415-775-1055
◪ Mexican siblings that offer "healthy, yuppie burritos", "fish tacos" and "tasty quesadillas"; the SOMA locale is "good for a refuel while clubbing", though a few complain about "small portions" and "bad service"; at least they're "cheap and quick."

Washington Square Bar & Grill S M 18 | 18 | 18 | $27
1707 Powell St. (Union St.), 415-982-8123
◪ Though Ed Moose has moved across the square, this venerable North Beach grill is "still alive and kicking"; "mediocre food" is secondary to the "lively upbeat atmosphere", "friendly service" and "fun bar" where all the drunks are "good drunks"; most agree this "casual old shoe" still has plenty of soul.

Waterfront Restaurant, The S M 19 | 22 | 18 | $29
Pier 7 (Embarcadero, Broadway), 415-391-2696
■ A "nicely done tourist trap", this Wharf seafooder provides "dependable" but "not memorable" fare and "good wines by the glass" in "a comfortable setting" with "a spectacular view of the bay"; "great for brunch" though "a bit costly for what it is."

Wente Bros. Restaurant S M 26 | 27 | 25 | $36
5050 Arroyo Rd. (Wente Bros. Sparkling Wine Cellars), Livermore, 510-447-3696
■ A "fantastic wine list" and lovely "vineyard setting" win acclaim at this "bright spot in the Livermore area"; the Californian cuisine ranges from "good" to "excellent", with "estate-raised beef" and "fabulous vegetarian dishes if requested"; it's a trip, but worth it for special occasions and the "unsurpassed" Sunday brunch.

Woodward's Garden S ⊄ 26 | 13 | 23 | $31

1700 Mission St. (Duboce St.), 415-621-7122

■ "Tiny" Mission New American that has fans cheering "hurray for women chefs" – Postrio and Greens alumnae Margie Conard and Dana Tommasino, whose "fabulous", "creative and wholesome" food served in cramped quarters is clearly "a labor of love"; the only drawback is a location with "noisy highway traffic overhead"; the "limited menu" changes weekly, so regulars return often to see how this garden grows.

Wu Kong S M 23 | 18 | 18 | $25

One Rincon Center, 101 Spear St. (bet. Howard & Mission Sts.), 415-957-9300

■ Some "unusual" Shanghai treats make the scene at this SOMA Chinese; "beautiful, flavorful food" and "exotic dim sum" earn high praise; but "watch out for indifferent waiters" because they won't watch out for you.

Yamato Restaurant & Sushi Bar S ▽ 19 | 19 | 21 | $26

717 California St. (Grant Ave.), 415-397-3456

◪ This Chinatown Japanese may be "a little tired", but it still has "well-prepared" donburi, sukiyaki and tempura; the sushi is "good for lunch" and "reliable" – so is the service, but "if only they spoke more English."

Yank Sing M 25 | 18 | 19 | $20

427 Battery St. (bet. Clay & Washington), 415-781-1111 S

49 Stevenson St. (bet. 1st & 2nd Sts.), 415-495-4510

■ "The best dim sum in SF" rolls your way at these "sublime" Downtown Chinese siblings; regulars advise "sit near the kitchen to get the best choice while it's hot"; some servings "can be greasy", but "the luck of the cart" is leveraged in your favor by a "well-prepared", "well-thought-out" selection that's "hard to stop eating"; so watch out, "the bill adds up fast."

Yet Wah S M 14 | 12 | 13 | $18

Pier 39, Fisherman's Wharf (Embarcadero), 415-434-4430

2140 Clement St. (23rd Ave.), 415-387-8040

2019 Larkspur Landing Circle (Sir Francis Drake Blvd.), Larkspur, 415-461-3631

■ "Yet why?" is the question most asked about this "uninspired formula franchise" serving "mass-produced", "American-style Chinese dishes"; given the "bland food" with service and decor to match, "plastic city" doesn't just mean they take credit cards – "boring then sum."

Yoshida-Ya S M | 23 | 20 | 20 | $26

2909 Webster St. (Union St.), 415-346-3431

■ "Stylish" Union Street Japanese that serves "excellent sushi", "yummi yakitori" and "consistently good" seafood dishes; you'll "love the little hibachis" on which you grill meats and vegetables before dipping them in savory sauces; less popular are sometimes "surly waiters" who leave diners feeling skewered.

Yoshi's Japanese Restaurant S M | 20 | 18 | 18 | $22

6030 Claremont Ave. (College Ave.), Oakland, 510-652-9200

■ Enjoy "good sushi", "delicious grilled fish", "outstanding" live jazz and service to match at this long- playing Oakland Japanese; the new "entertainment menu" also lets you get "lost in the blues" while swallowing your yellowfin.

Yuet Lee S M | 23 | 3 | 11 | $16

1300 Stockton St. (Broadway), 415-982-6020 ◐

3601 26th St. (bet. Valencia & Guerrero Sts.), 415-550-8998

◪ "Always crowded and noisy" Chinatown "dives" offering the "best Chinese for those late-night cravings"; just focus on the "great seafood" and "fabulous noodles" and forget about the "meat-freezer" decor.

Yujean's Modern Cuisine of China S | 24 | 14 | 19 | $23

843 San Pablo Ave. (Solano Ave.), Albany, 510-525-8557

◪ Many dishes are "innovative" and the wine list is "one of the best" at this East Bay "gourmet Chinese" (try the "unreal tea-smoked duck"); but a few carp that as "prices go up, quality comes down."

Zachary's Chicago Pizza S M ⌿ | 25 | 10 | 14 | $13

5801 College Ave. (Oak Grove St.), Oakland, 510-655-6385

1853 Solano Ave. (Fresno) Berkeley, 510-525-5950

■ "The best", "excellent", "wonderful" are just some of the raves for these highly rated East Bay pizzerias; if it's deep-dish pizza you're looking for, there's "no need to fly to Chicago"; N.B. many surveyors say the "stuffed- spinach-and-mushroom" pie is a "fab" "classic."

Zax | 26 | 22 | 23 | $30

2330 Taylor St. (Columbus Ave.), 415-563-6266

■ "Charming" North Beach Mediterranean newcomer that's a bit "off the path but worth the hunt"; the small menu is well-put-together, and "friendly if uneven service" delivers food that's "delicious without being heavily sauced"; the "limited wine list and high corkage fee" ensure you won't be heavily sauced either.

ZUNI CAFE ◐ S | 25 | 21 | 19 | $31

1658 Market St. (bet. Gough & Franklin Sts.), 415-552-2522

◪ "Funky, fun and full of attitude", this "très SF" Civic Center Eclectic-Mediterranean is "great for people-watching" and "best at lunch"; the "creative menu" still delivers ("excellent polenta", "best roast chicken", "always delicious Zuni burgers"), too bad the "rude" waiters sometimes don't; the "interesting clientele" is part of the hip decor – strike a pose and slide some "great oysters" at the bar.

Zza's Trattoria S M | 18 | 14 | 17 | $20

552 Grand Ave. (Euclid), Oakland, 510-839-9124

■ Finally, a "children's neighborhood restaurant" that serves good food along with the crayons; there's "great pizza", "family fun" and "friendly service", but if you don't enjoy dining with kids, stay home.

North of San Francisco

	F	D	S	C
AUBERGE DU SOLEIL S M	25	28	25	$47

Auberge Du Soleil Inn, 180 Rutherford Hill Rd. (Silverado Trail), Rutherford, 707-963-1211
◪ The bright Napa *soleil* is one of the most reliable features at this hotel charmer, where a "romantic" French meal on the "heavenly outdoor deck" feels like "vacationing in the south of France"; despite high ratings, some find the culinary forecast iffy, with "fussy, overrated" and "pricey" food; yet even they enjoy the "best view in the valley" augmented by a bottle from the "impressive wine list."

	F	D	S	C
Bistro Don Giovanni S M	24	24	24	$31

4110 St. Helena Hwy. (Salvador St.), Napa, 707-244-3300
■ The "warmth of the staff" and vineyard views make this "lively" Italian bistro (on the site of the former Table 29) a pleasant Napa roadside stop; you also get "wholesome", "consistently good food"; "Mozart would be pleased."

	F	D	S	C
Brava Terrace S M	24	23	22	$33

3010 St. Helena Hwy. N. (Lodi Lane), St. Helena, 707-963-9300
■ Chef Fred Halpert's Californian-French bistro wins *bravi* for its terrace and its "Napa paradise" setting offering "magnificent outdoor dining among the redwoods"; a frequently changing menu of carefully prepared, "gutsy" food is paired with a "great wine list"; for some, the spell is broken by "unprofessional" service.

	F	D	S	C
Cafe Beaujolais S M ⇏	26	22	23	$30

961 Ukiah St. (Evergreen St.), Mendocino, 707-937-5614
◪ For nearly two decades, Margaret Fox's "cozy, romantic, country-style" restaurant with an Eclectic- International menu has been a culinary mecca on the North Coast; as with any legend, it "doesn't live up to its reputation" for some, but all agree it provides great baked goods and the "best breakfasts anywhere."

	F	D	S	C
California Cafe Bar & Grill S M	21	20	21	$24

Village Shopping Ctr., 1736 Redwood Hwy. (Paradise Dr.), Corte Madera, 415-924-2233
1540 N. California Blvd. (Civic St.), Walnut Creek, 510-938-9977
Stanford Barn, 700 Welch Rd. (Quarry St.), Palo Alto, 415-325-2233

California Cafe Bar & Grill (Cont.)
Valley Fair Shopping Ctr., 2855 Stevens Creek Blvd. (Winchester Ave.), Santa Clara, 408-296-2233
Old Town Shopping Ctr., 50 University Ave. (bet. Main St. & Hwy. 9), Los Gatos, 408-354-8118
◪ The chain reaction is mixed: devotees praise these Californians as "surprisingly good for a chain" with "fresh, reliable food, attentive service" and "moderate" prices; critics say the "cookie-cutter formula" produces food that's "a little tired" and "clichéd"; maybe they're both right.

Catahoula Restaurant & Saloon S M | 25 | 23 | 21 | $35 |
Mount View Hotel, 1457 Lincoln Ave. (Washington Ave.), Calistoga, 707-942-2275
■ Down-home up North: chef-owner Jan Birnbaum's (ex Campton Place) Louisiana roots stretch out at this "exciting", new Southern feeding and watering hole that's a "welcome change from Mediterranean" in Napa; while "not authentic" to diehards, surveyors praise his "unusual pairings of textures and spices" and the "communal table for singles" at this lively "place to be seen and not heard."

CHATEAU SOUVERAIN S | 24 | 27 | 23 | $37 |
400 Souverain Rd. (Hwy. 101, Independence Lane exit), 707-433-3141
◪ Many lament the restyling of a once-elegant restaurant into a "romantic" yet casual Californian cafe, saying the food, though "good", is no longer "superb"; but it's still set in a Sonoma winery that looks like a French chateau, and the total experience – from "gorgeous location" to "great wine values" – makes it "occasionally worth the trip."

DOMAINE CHANDON S M | 28 | 27 | 26 | $42 |
1 California Dr. (Hwy. 29), Yountville, 707-944-2892
■ The food and service, "rustic" setting and, for certain, the wine all "sparkle" at this Napa Valley Contemporary French in the midst of a stunning vineyard and winery; as always, a few are "not impressed", but everyone else agrees this is a "regal dining experience" right through the "amazing desserts" and the "best splurge in Napa."

Downtown Bakery & Creamery S M ⊄ | 28 | 14 | 18 | $9 |
308-A Center St. (on the Plaza), Healdsburg, 707-431-2719
■ Locals love this simple bakery and coffee stand co-founded by pastry chef Lindsey Shere of Chez Panisse; the take-out-only fare includes some of the "best baked goods in Northern California" ("hard to imagine better baguettes, scones or sticky buns") as well as "great" house-made ice cream, making this a "best pit stop on the Sonoma wine trail."

Eastside Oyster Bar & Grill S M — 23 | 19 | 20 | $32

127 E. Napa St. (First St.), Sonoma, 707-939-1266

◪ There are enough pearls on chef Charles Saunders' "fresh and imaginative" menu to make this seafooder "one of the best choices in Sonoma", although a few carp about "dinky portions" and "disoriented, amateurish service"; given the too-small, always-packed dining room, regulars prefer the "charming outdoor patio for a summer treat."

Foothill Cafe S — 24 | 10 | 23 | $23

2766 Old Sonoma Rd. (Foothill Blvd.), Napa, 707-252-6178

■ Don't be put off by the strip-mall location or modest decor of this Napa "neighborhood jewel", an American grill serving "good home-cooked meals"; the BBQ ribs and other entrees from the oakwood smoker are surefire hits.

FRENCH LAUNDRY, THE S — 27 | 26 | 26 | $48

6640 Washington St. (Creek Ave.), Yountville, 707-944-2380

■ A recent ownership change and the arrival of chef Thomas Keller add luster to this "charming Napa escape" where "extremely fresh" Eclectic–New American fare is "cooked to perfection"; it's a "memorable experience" that's like being a "pampered" "guest in someone's home."

Grille S M — ▽ 27 | 25 | 26 | $35

Sonoma Mission Inn, 18140 Hwy. 12 (Boyes Blvd.), Boyes Hot Springs, 707-939-2415

■ A treatment at the spa, of course, makes everything seem blissfully "unbelievable", including the "zesty, imaginative" food at this Californian grill; set in the "lovely, peaceful" Sonoma Mission Inn, the harshest food criticism it gets is "not quite great but very proficient."

John Ash & Co. S — 26 | 26 | 26 | $40

4330 Barnes Rd. (bet. Hwy. 101 & River Rd.), Santa Rosa, 707-527-7687

◪ There's more company and less John Ash at this "beautiful", pricey Californian since Ash shifted from chef to menu consultant, but there's still "great care" in the preparation and serving of "wonderful", "innovative food"; lustier palates crave "a little more spice with the thought", but the consensus is this mecca on the "lovely" grounds of a Sonoma vineyard remains "one of California's finest."

Kenwood Restaurant S — 27 | 23 | 24 | $32

9900 Hwy. 12 (Warm Springs Rd.), Kenwood, 707-833-6326

■ A "hidden treasure", this Sonoma French-American bistro is popular among locals for its relaxed style, "excellent, unpretentious food" and "patio overlooking a vineyard"; the duck, rabbit and venison come highly recommended, and don't miss the "to-die-for sweetbread salad."

Madrona Manor Restaurant S M 24 | 25 | 22 | $40

Madrona Manor, 1001 Westside Rd. (bet. Mill St. & W. Dry Creek Rd.), Healdsburg, 707-433-4231

◪ The "exquisite, romantic setting" and "hospitable service" at this Sonoma Cal-Eclectic in a Victorian inn make it a "wonderful destination" with "outstanding" cuisine; a few critics claim that food and atmosphere are "going downhill", and even fans agree that prices are headed up the mountain.

Meadowood Grill S M – | – | – | M

Meadowood Resort, 900 Meadowood Lane, St. Helena, 707-963-3646

At this airy, country-style bistro in Napa's Meadowood resort, chef Fabrice Marcon prepares a fantastic breakfast buffet and simple but tasty dinner menu that ranges from Dungeness crab cakes and lightly 'cued salmon to grilled rib-eye; spa-goers will appreciate the healthy options.

Meadowood Restaurant S M 24 | 27 | 24 | $44

Meadowood Resort, 900 Meadowood Lane (Silverado Trail), St. Helena, 800-458-8080

◪ Set in a posh resort, this Napa Provençal serves "elegant food in a fantastic setting"; it has its critics ("overpriced", "pretentious", "so-so"), but high ratings confirm that most diners enthuse over this "romantic" destination.

Mustards Grill S M 26 | 21 | 23 | $30

7399 St. Helena Hwy., Napa, 707-944-2424

■ For Napa visitors and locals alike, this immensely popular grill remains "a must"; "another Cindy Pawlcyn success story", this "unpretentious" roadside bistro with a "wide variety of foods and prices" "epitomizes California cuisine without the silliness"; reserve well in advance.

Napa Valley Wine Train S M 21 | 26 | 22 | $45

1275 McKinstry St. (1st St.), Napa, 800-427-4124

◪ An "enjoyable", "moving experience", not only for the "pretty good" Californian-Continental fare but for the chance to dine in an "amazingly restored" antique train that travels through 14 miles of wine country; it's "the closest thing to the Orient Express in California", including the price tag.

Pasta Prego Trattoria S M 23 | 18 | 22 | $25

Grapeyard Shopping Ctr., 3206 Jefferson St. (bet. Trancas & Pueblo Sts.), Napa, 707-224-9011

Fusilli Ristorante

620 Jackson St. (W. Texas St.), Fairfield, 707-428-4211

■ "A little-known pasta jewel" tucked away in a strip mall, this Napa Italian is a "good value" that's "solid, easy, and reliable"; "outside dining adds to the experience" and the lively ambiance and open kitchen make this a family favorite; its Fairfield sibling shares many of the same qualities.

Piatti S M 23 | 23 | 22 | $28

6480 Washington St. (Oak Circle), Yountville, 707-944-2070
Eldorado Hotel, 405 First St. W. (Spain St.), Sonoma, 707-996-2351
Stanford Shop. Ctr., 180 El Camino Real, Palo Alto, 415-324-9733

The original Yountville (Napa) and Sonoma Italians have given birth to six bambini throughout California including a Palo Alto branch; though a few criticize "franchise mediocrity", legions of fans say they're "reliable" examples of "formula places that really work"; "terrific" pastas, pizzas and garlic bread are the signatures here, along with "roast chicken to kill for."

Samba Java S M 19 | 18 | 18 | $25

109A Plaza St. (bet. Center & Healdsburg Aves.), Healdsburg, 707-433-5282

"A must if you're in Healdsburg", this "zany" Cal-Carib-Eclectic features "spicy original cooking" and "whimsical" combinations, with "good burgers" for the less adventurous; everyone gets to try the "uncomfortable chairs."

Showley's At Miramonte S 24 | 20 | 24 | $33

1327 Railroad Ave. (bet. Hunt & Adams Sts.), St. Helena, 707-963-1200

"Friendly owners" and "personalized service" win high praise at this "charming, homey" Napa Cal-Eclectic with French and Italian influences; the "improving" food is "always better than expected" – some even say "excellent."

Stars Oakville Cafe S M 22 | 18 | 20 | $32

7848 St. Helena Hwy. 29 (Oakville Crossroad), Oakville, 707-944-8905

Another sparkler in Jeremiah (Stars, Stars Cafe) Tower's constellation, this small Napa New American "is coming along" but still has "a few rough edges"; though mostly "outstanding", the "limited menu" can be "inconsistent" and is served by a "disorganized" staff amidst "stark decor" that lacks luster; but there's "great fritto misto" and "sandwiches are sure winners."

TERRA S M 28 | 27 | 26 | $41

1345 Railroad Ave. (bet. Hunt & Adams Sts.), St. Helena, 707-963-8931

The highest-rated restaurant in wine country, this Napa Eclectic stakes its claim with an "incredibly inventive and creative" kitchen and a "calming, simple, charming, rustic interior"; chef Hiro Sone is "a magician at combining flavors" from Northern Italy, Southern France and, occasionally, Japan in his "unique California cooking"; "Hiro is my hero."

TRA VIGNE S M 26 | 28 | 24 | $33

1050 Charter Oak Ave. (Hwy. 29), St. Helena, 707-963-4444

■ The "quintessential Tuscan villa" atmosphere at this Napa Cal-Italian is practically irresistible, and so is the "wonderfully robust" food (try "fresh figs and prosciutto", "delicious pastas, polenta and house-cured olives"); there's a "large, bustling dining room", but many prefer a table on the "idyllic outdoor patio" among the vines; all in all, this will be your "easiest trip to Italy."

Tre Scalini M 23 | 18 | 20 | $34

241 Healdsburg Ave. (Matheson St.), Healdsburg, 707-433-1772

◪ A local favorite, this "cozy Northern Italian with spirit" brings a bit of Tuscany to the Sonoma wine country; rack of lamb, "good pastas and grilled items" are touted, though some think the menu "doesn't meet the competition"; most find the formal service "attentive", but a few say "stuffy."

Trilogy S 25 | 19 | 22 | $38

1234 Main St. (Hunt St.), St. Helena, 707-963-5507

■ Three's a crowd at this "favorite Napa Valley spot for two"; it's "a special room for romantic dinners" where patrons adore the "incredible", "inexpensive wine list" and "consistently excellent" Californian–French Classic food, though several disappointed bread lovers find the house French *pain* a pain.

South of San Francisco

	F	D	S	C

Beausejour S M ▽ 23 | 21 | 20 | $30

170 State St. (3rd St.), Los Altos, 415-948-1382

◪ Fans say the original chef's son-in-law "carries on a magnificent tradition" producing "good, steady" New French food at this Peninsula shopping-mall locale; critics say it's "stuck in a time warp" with service varying from "very good to grouchy."

Campbell House S ▽ 29 | 20 | 28 | $39

106 E. Campbell Ave. (bet. 3rd & 4th Sts.), Campbell, 408-374-5757

◪ A "house full of culinary love", this "romantic" New American serves "great duck and rack of lamb" (only the "desserts need work"); there's "friendly" service and a "warm" setting (though it's "too small and quiet" for some), and the prix fixe menu is a "good value."

Casanova S M 24 | 25 | 23 | $34

Fifth Ave. (San Carlos St.), Carmel, 408-625-0501

■ A "popular" Italian-French "charmer" that lives up to its name – "the most romantic restaurant in Carmel" – with "good", "reliable" food and a "great wine list" adding to the pleasure; "lunch is heaven" on the patio.

Central 159 M 27 | 18 | 22 | $30

529 Central Ave. (15th St., bet. Lighthouse & Central Aves.), Pacific Grove, 408-655-4280

■ "Creative, high-quality food" and "careful attention to customers" keep this Monterey-area Californian popular even after moving to a "hard-to-find", "institutional" location; "tables are tight" and the lights "too bright", but maybe they're a navigational aid; it's definitely "worth the hunt."

Chef Chu's Inc. S M 22 | 16 | 17 | $22

1067 N. San Antonio Rd. (El Camino Real), Los Altos, 415-948-2696

◪ Expect "scrumptious" "New Year's shrimp" and the "best lemon chicken" at this "large, busy" Peninsula Chinese, especially when Chu himself is in the kitchen; though some say it's too "Americanized" and "rushed", most diners rave about "one of the classiest Chinese restaurants around."

Chez Renee ▽ 28 | 28 | 28 | $33

9051 Soquel Dr. (Rio del Mar), Aptos, 408-688-5566

■ A "winner" in a Santa Cruz redwood grove, this "intimate" Cal-French-Eclectic offers fine food "with a French-Italian flair", "great prices" and "wonderful service" (the charming Renee herself will guide you to your table); "if this restaurant were in SF, you'd need to reserve a month in advance."

Club XIX S M 24 | 25 | 22 | $39

Lodge at Pebble Beach, 17 Mile Dr. (18th Green at The Pebble Beach Golf Links), Pebble Beach, 408-625-8519

■ "If you want classy on the Monterey Peninsula", this French country "hunting lodge" has "excellent food on the terrace", "super views" and an "elegant, clubby feel" (though that means "stuffy" to some).

Covey Restaurant, The S M 26 | 26 | 27 | $46

Quail Lodge Resort & Golf Club, 8205 Valley Greens Dr. (Carmel Valley Rd.), Carmel, 408-624-1581

◪ "Small, great, beautiful" sums up this "expensive" Californian-Continental in Carmel with "excellent" food and staff; although the "first-class country-club atmosphere" can be a "little stodgy", isn't that the idea?

Crow's Nest S M 16 | 21 | 17 | $21

2218 E. Cliff Dr. (Lake Ave.), Santa Cruz, 408-476-4560

■ If "good bar food" and a terrific ocean view are all you need, you'll crow about your "afternoon on the deck" at this American steakhouse/seafooder; if you're looking for better than "edible", look elsewhere.

EMILE'S RESTAURANT 28 | 25 | 26 | $43

545 S. Second St. (William St.), San Jose, 408-289-1960

■ The "best restaurant in San Jose" offers a "creative", "ever-changing" Contemporary French menu with an "excellent low-fat selection"; occasional rants about "crowded tables" and "petite portions for the price" are outnumbered by raves for the "new decor" that "greatly improved ambiance" and "fab specials."

ERNA'S ELDERBERRY HOUSE S M 29 | 28 | 29 | $56

48688 Victoria Lane (Hwy. 41), Oakhurst, 209-683-6800

■ On the road to Yosemite, save your appetite and your money for this Cal-French "oasis" that's "plucked from another place and time" and offers "wonderful everything"; expect "unusual twists on traditional dishes" and a "lovely dining experience"; it's 3½ hours from SF, but happily there are rooms at the inn.

Eulipia S | 25 | 19 | 21 | $28 |

374 S. First St. (bet. San Carlos & San Salvador Sts.), San Jose, 408-280-6161

"There's always something good" at this "fresh and easy" Cal-American with "various ethnic touches" (steaks to Mexican to pasta); many suggest it for "after-theater" dining, though a few say "little real quality", "for yuppies" and "needs warmth"; still, ratings support the claim that it's "well worth the trip to San Jose."

FRESH CREAM S M | 27 | 25 | 26 | $43 |

Heritage Harbor, 99 Pacific St., Ste. 100C (Scott St.), Monterey, 408-375-9798

When visiting this Monterey modern "don't miss the milk-shake dessert in a chocolate bag" – but first there's the "exquisite" dinner: "Contemporary French at its best" that's "rich, sinfully delicious" and "a work of art"; the "service couldn't be better" and the "gorgeous new dining room" has "a great bay view"; despite these pluses, a few say "overrated" and wonder "why the hoopla?"

Fung Lum S M | 19 | 23 | 20 | $23 |

1815 S. Bascom Ave. (bet. Hamilton & Campbell Aves.), Campbell, 408-377-6955

"Take mom" to this "upscale" San Jose Cantonese; it's "slipped a little", but "she'll love" the "stunning decor" and the "inauthentic", "1950s-style Chinese food" will go down ok, provided you pick up the check.

Gervais ▽ 21 | 20 | 23 | $34 |

1798 Park Ave. (Naglee), San Jose, 408-275-8631

A few ask "what's the big deal?" about this Classic French in San Jose; maybe they don't agree with admirers of the "wonderful staff and owner" and instead think they're "snooty"; the place might be "not as great as Emile's", but "it's worth going back" for its year-after-year "excellence."

La Forêt S ▽ 25 | 26 | 24 | $44 |

21747 Bertram Rd. (Almaden Rd.), San Jose, 408-997-3458

It's "worth the trip for the venison alone" to this "romantic" Contemporary French creekside hideaway in San Jose specializing in "wonderful" meat and game dishes; the food "hovers on the edge of excellence" and "the ambiance makes it special."

La Mère Michelle S ▽ 22 | 23 | 25 | $43 |

14467 Big Basin Way (3rd St.), Saratoga, 408-867-5272

Opinions divide on this French-Continental near San Jose: for most it's "romantic, real, and tasty", with "above-average desserts"; but a few detractors say "the red velvet decor is old, so is the food" and "there are better places for the price."

LE MOUTON NOIR S M 27 | 26 | 26 | $46

14560 Big Basin Way (4th St.), Saratoga, 408-867-7017

There's just enough "innovation" on the "pleasing menu" at this South Bay French charmer to set it apart from the traditional herd; some wish the "crowded tables" also were "further apart", but most find the "intimate dining" in a "cozy, pretty bungalow" to their liking; it's "very California", where black sheep make good.

Le Papillon S M 26 | 22 | 23 | $36

410 Saratoga Ave. (Kiely Blvd.), San Jose, 408-296-3730

"Excellent always", this San Jose New French offers "awesome food and service", though a few flutter that it's not "authentic gourmet, but a nice South Bay imitation"; for best results "get a waiter who speaks English", but the Grand Marnier soufflé is good in any language.

Lion & Compass M 23 | 23 | 21 | $32

1023 N. Fair Oaks Ave. (Weddell), Sunnyvale, 408-745-1260

Lead your safari to this "reliable" San Jose New American "power-lunch palace" and take your bytes with "Silicon Valley's who's who" – but if that's not your style, you may find this in-spot "overrated and expensive", with only "wonderful fish and desserts" to roar about.

Los Gatos Brewing Co. S M 22 | 24 | 21 | $23

130 N. Santa Cruz Ave., Ste. G, Los Gatos, 408-395-9929

Smart cats "go for the brews" and the "good pizza and pasta" in this "open, noisy, fun" Los Gatos brewpub; but while its admirers purr about the "tasty bar food" and "innovative menu", others cry that "disastrous" dinners are "a waste of money" – hey, chill out!

Pacific Fresh S M 18 | 16 | 16 | $22

1130 N. Mathilda Ave. (Lockheed Way), Sunnyvale, 408-745-1710

550 Ellinwood Way (Contracosta Blvd.), Pleasant Hill, 510-827-3474

This "surprisingly good" San Jose fish franchise offers "decent seafood" at "reasonable prices"; fans laud the "great salmon" and extensive wine list, but not everyone agrees: "these places give fish a bad name."

PACIFIC'S EDGE S M 28 | 28 | 26 | $46

Highlands Inn, Hwy. 1, Carmel, 408-624-0471

Eat-inn in the pines overlooking the Pacific at this "all-around-wonderful" Californian; the "delightfully interesting menu" offers "the best seafood" and a "fabulous prix fixe" option; a few grumble that the service is "stuffy", but most find it "solicitous" and feel "catered to in all ways"; the most serious complaint may be that "you can't eat the view."

Palermo S M | 22 | 19 | 20 | $25 |

394 S. Second St. (San Carlos Ave.), San Jose, 408-297-0607

◪ Comments on this relocated San Jose Italian are all over the map: to some it's like "a trip to Sicily" with "excellent pasta", "good roast chicken" and "addictive" bread; but others say "food and service went downhill" when it "moved to a larger, ornate" setting.

Paolo's Restaurant M | 26 | 26 | 24 | $36 |

333 W. San Carlos St. #150 (bet. Almaden Blvd. & Woz Way), San Jose, 408-294-2558

■ "Wonderful" South Bay Italian that offers a "romantic setting" complete with art collection, and a menu you can't refuse featuring "wonderful desserts"; budget-watchers note that it can add up, especially if you let them "substitute a more expensive wine"; do yourself a favor and "start with the famous antipasto."

Pasta Moon M | 24 | 16 | 19 | $28 |

315 Main St. (Mill St.), Half Moon Bay, 415-726-5125 S
Oyster Point Marina Inn, 425 Marina Blvd. (Oyster Point Blvd.), So. San Francisco, 415-876-7090

■ These "down-home", "crowded" Italians have fans baying with delight over their "great view" and pastas that are among "the best on the coast" albeit "pricey"; each of these "garlic-lovers' delights" has its partisans, and many "love them both."

Plumed Horse, The M | 25 | 23 | 24 | $42 |

14555 Big Basin Way (4th St.), Saratoga, 408-867-4711

◪ "Dark, romantic" San Jose French-American that provides a "good start for a tryst", or at least will "make you feel special"; it offers "wonderful food for the wealthy" and "the best wine list in the Bay Area", though a few object to the "stuffy crowd"; still, the majority rules: this is where to take her – or him.

Rio Grill S M | 24 | 21 | 22 | $30 |

Crossroads Shopping Ctr., 101 Crossroads Blvd. (Rio Rd.), Carmel Valley, 408-625-5436

■ "Bravo!" for this "always fun" Carmel Cal-Eclectic, where "kids are welcome" amid the "lively, high-energy crowd"; the "reliable" menu includes "wonderful ribs" and artichokes that alone "are worth the drive from SF"; while a few say "not the same without Cindy" (Pawlcyn), it's still a carnival for most.

San Benito House S ▽ 22 | 24 | 21 | $29

356 Main St. (Mill St.), Half Moon Bay, 415-726-3425

■ A "lovely country inn" in Half Moon Bay, this "warm" Mediterranean-Eclectic offers "a small, imaginative menu" that's "excellent when it's right" (and ratings show it often is); weather permitting, you'll have a "nice terrace lunch", one more reason why fans plead "please don't tell anyone."

Sardine Factory S M 19 | 20 | 20 | $38

701 Wave St. (Prescott St.), Monterey, 408-373-3775

◪ This Cannery Row landmark still packs the tourists into its "opulent" (some say "pretentious") dining room for "hearty Italian" fare; admirers like the "delicious if pricey" abalone and the "great wine list", but they may be swayed by the view: to others, it's only "a cut above Denny's."

Sierra Mar S M ▽ 25 | 29 | 25 | $48

Post Ranch Inn, Hwy. 1 (25 miles south of Carmel), Big Sur, 408-667-2800

■ The "breathtaking ocean view and super cuisine" make this Californian a "new hot spot" in Big Sur; even if the "internationally influenced" menu is "a little far-out", it's kept rooted by a "great wine cellar"; at its best, the "whole experience" can be "incomparable", but several raters caution: "go when the main chef is cooking."

Sunset Dining Room, The S M ▽ 18 | 25 | 22 | $33

Chaminade at Santa Cruz, 1 Chaminade Lane (bet. Paul Sweet Rd. & Soquel Dr.), Santa Cruz, 408-475-5600

■ Go for the sunset and skip the dining, sums up comments on this Peninsula hotel International seafooder – though a "great brunch", "friendly" staff and Friday-night seafood buffets are bright spots on the horizon; even so, "dull, heavy-handed" fare causes some to conclude that it's "corporation-run and it shows."

Tarpy's Roadhouse S M 23 | 22 | 21 | $30

2999 Monterey-Salinas Hwy. 68 (3 miles east of Hwy. 1), Monterey, 408-647-1444

■ "Good, new addition to the Peninsula scene" serving "imaginative" Californian-American cuisine in a "beautiful setting" – a "unique stone building" with pleasant outdoor seating; service can be "too casual" for some, but most say it's "a must when in Monterey" and worth the road trip when you're not.

INDEXES TO RESTAURANTS

SPECIAL FEATURES AND APPEALS

TYPES OF CUISINE*

Afghan

Helmand

American (New)

Acorn Tea
A La Carte
Avenue Grill
Boulevard
Cafe/All Seasons
Cafe 222
Campbell House/S
Campton Place
Caprice, The
Carnelian Room
Cheer's Cafe
Club 181
Courtyard B & G
Cypress Club
Doidge's
Eddie Rickenbacker's
ERIC Restaurant
Eulipia/S
Fog City Diner
Fournou's Ovens
French Laundry/N
Grille/N
Ivy's
JoAnn's B Street
JoAnn's Cafe
Johnny Love's
Kenwood/N
Kim's
Lark Creek Inn
La Scene
Lion & Compass/S
Los Gatos/S
Mama's Royal Cafe
Max's Opera Cafe
Mo's Burgers
One Market
Park Grill
Pauli's Cafe
Pier 23 Cafe
Plumed Horse/S
Ritz-Carlton Din. Rm.
Rivoli Restaurant
Rotunda, The
Sally's
Stars
Stars Cafe
Stars Oakville/N
Tarpy's Roadhouse/S
Woodward's Garden

American (Regional)

Eastside Oyster/N
Foothill Cafe/N
Gate Five
Gulf Coast G & B

American (Traditional)

Annabelle's
Big Four
Bix
Buchanan Grill
Buffalo Grill
Cal. Roastery
Carrara's Cafe
Clark's by Bay
Clement St. B & G
Cliff House
Crow's Nest/S
Delancey St.
Fat Apple's
Fly Trap
Garden Court
Gordon Biersch
Hamburger Mary's
Hard Rock Cafe
Harris'
Harry Denton's
MacArthur Park
Mama's
Max's Diner
Mel's Drive-In
Pacific T & G
Paragon
Perry's

* All restaurants are in the San Francisco metropolitan area unless otherwise noted (N = North of San Francisco and S = South of San Francisco).

Sam's Anchor
Sam's Grill
Sand Dollar
Sears Fine Foods
Trio Cafe
U.S. Restaurant
Vic Stewart's

Asian

Crustacean
Ginger Island

Bakeries

Downtown Bakery/N
Fat Apple's
Sally's

Bar-B-Q

Barnaby's By Bay
Buckeye Roadhse.
Doug's BBQ
MacArthur Park

Brazilian

Bahia

Burmese

Mandalay
Nan Yang

Cafeterias

Tommy's Joynt

Cajun/Creole

Blue Light
Elite Cafe, The
PJ's Oyster Bed
Regina's

Californian

Ace Cafe
Act IV
A. Sabella's
Balboa Cafe
Bay Wolf
Brava Terrace/N
Bridges
Cactus Cafe
Cafe Adriano
Cafe Akimbo
Cafe Chez Panisse
Cafe Flore
Cafe Kati
Cal. Cul. Academy
California Cafe/N
Cal. Pizza Kit.
Caprice, The
Cava 555
Central 159/S
Chateau Souverain/N
Chez Panisse
China Moon Cafe
Courtyard B & G
Covey, The/S
Curbside Cafe
El Paseo
Erna's House/S
Eulipia/S
Flea St. Cafe
French Room
Garibaldi
Grille/N
Hayes St. Grill
Horizons
Island Cafe
John Ash & Co./N
Julie's
Kelly's on Trinity
Little City
London Wine Bar
Madrona Manor/N
Maxfield's B & G
Meadowood Grill/N
Meadowood Rest./N
Moose's
Mustards Grill/N
Napa Vall. Wine/N
Narsai's Cafe
O Chame
Omnivore
Pacific
Pacific's Edge/S
Panama Hotel
Park Grill
Pat O'Shea's
Pavilion
Postrio
Rio Grill/S
Ritz-Carlton Din. Rm.
Ritz-Carlton Terr.

Roti
Santa Fe B & G
Savannah Grill
Showley's/N
Sierra Mar/S
Splendido's
Square One
Stanford Park
Station House
Tarpy's Roadhouse/S
Tra Vigne/N
Trilogy/N
Victor's
Wente Bros.

Cambodian

Angkor Wat
Phnom Penh

Caribbean

Caribbean Zone
Cha Cha Cha's
Geva's
Miss Pearl's Jam
Primo Patio Cafe

Chinese

Brandy Ho's
Chef Chu's/S
China House
China Moon Cafe
Empress of China
Eric's Chinese
Flower Lounge
Fountain Court
Fung Lum/S
Harbor Village
House of Nanking
Hunan Rest.
Imperial Palace
Jade Villa
Jin Jiang Kee Joon
King of China
Kirin
Lichee Garden
Long Life Vegi Hse.
Mandarin House
Mandarin, The
Mayflower
North Sea Village
Ocean Restaurant
South China Cafe
Tommy Toy's
Ton Kiang
Wu Kong
Yank Sing
Yet Wah
Yuet Lee
Yujean's

Coffee Shops/Diners

Bette's Oceanview
Dottie's Cafe
Fog City Diner
Gray Whale
JoAnn's B Street
JoAnn's Cafe
Mama's Royal Cafe
Max's Diner
Sears Fine Foods

Continental

Barbarossa
Bella Vista
Cafe de Bordeaux
Cafe Majestic
Cafe Mozart
Cal. Cul. Academy
Cal. Roastery
Carnelian Room
Covey, The/S
Dal Baffo
El Paseo
French Room
Jack's
Julius' Castle
La Mère Michelle/S
La Petite Auberge
Le Club
Mama's
Nadine's
Napa Vall. Wine/N
Nob Hill
Old Swiss House

Delis

Brother's Deli
Max's Opera Cafe
Narsai's Cafe
Saul's Deli
Vivande Porta Via

Dim Sum
Flower Lounge
Fountain Court
Fung Lum/S
Harbor Village
Imperial Palace
Jade Villa
Jin Jiang Kee Joon
King of China
Lichee Garden
Mandarin, The
Mayflower
North Sea Village
Ocean Restaurant
Ton Kiang
Wu Kong
Yank Sing

Eclectic
Cafe Beaujolais/N
Cafe Kati
Chez Renee/S
Embarko
Firefly
Flea St. Cafe
Flying Saucer
French Laundry/N
Ginger Island
Kiss
Madrona Manor/N
Occidental Grill
Panama Hotel
Pauline's Pizza
Rio Grill/S
Ruby's
Samba Java/N
San Benito Hse./S
Savannah Grill
Showley's/N
Square One
Station House
Terra/N
Thornhill Cafe
Woodward's Garden
Zuni Cafe

Ethiopian
Fana Ethiopian
Rasselas

French
Alta Mira
Auberge du Soleil/N
Brasserie Savoy
Cafe Fanny
Casanova/S
Downtown Bakery/N
Ernie's
Fleur de Lys
Fresh Cream/S
Gervais/S
La Petite Auberge
Le Club
Le Cyrano
Left Bank
L'Olivier
Rue de Main
Ti Couz
Tourelle Cafe
Trilogy/N
231 Ellsworth

French Bistro
Anjou
Baker St. Bistro
Bistro Clovis
Bistro M
Bizou
Brava Terrace/N
Cafe Bastille
Cafe Claude
Cafe Jacqueline
Cafe Maisonnette
Chambord
Chez Michel
Chez T.J.
Citron
City of Paris
Fringale
Kenwood/N
La Bergerie
L'Amie Donia
Le Central Bistro
L'Entrecote
Liberté
Metropole
Rosmarino
South Park Cafe

French (New)

Act IV
A La Carte
Alain Rondelli
Amelio's
Beausejour/S
Cafe Jacqueline
Chez T.J.
Citron
Club XIX/S
Domaine Chandon/N
El Paseo
Emile's/S
Erna's House/S
Fleur de Lys
Fresh Cream/S
Heights, The
La Folie
La Forêt/S
Le Marquis
Le Mouton Noir/S
Le Papillon/S
Le Trou
Masa's
Pacific
Plumed Horse/S
Rubicon
Sherman House
231 Ellsworth
Victor's

German

Schroeder's
Suppenkuche
Tommy's Joynt

Greek

Asimakopoulos

Hamburgers

Balboa Cafe
Bill's Place
Buchanan Grill
Clement St. B & G
Doidge's
Eddie Rickenbacker's
Fat Apple's
Gordon Biersch
Hamburger Mary's
Hard Rock Cafe
Mel's Drive-In
Mo's Burgers
Original Joe's
Perry's

Hawaiian

Avalon

Ice Cream Shops

JoAnn's B Street
JoAnn's Cafe

Indian

Appam
Gaylord Indian
India House
Indian Oven
Maharani India
North India

Indonesian

Rice Table

International

Cafe Beaujolais/N
Kiss
Sunset Dining Rm./S
Washington Sq. B & G

Italian

(N = Northern;
S = Southern;
N & S = includes both)

Acquerello (N)
Adriana's (N&S)
A La Carte (N&S)
Alexander (N)
Alioto's (S)
Allegro (N)
A. Sabella's (N&S)
Bacco (N&S)
Baci Caffe (N&S)
Barbarossa (N)
Bardelli's (N)
Basta Pasta (N)
Bella Voce (N)
Bistro D. Giovanni/N (N&S)
Bizou (N&S)
Bocce Cafe (N)
Bonta (N&S)

Buca Giovanni (N)
Bucci's (N&S)
Cafe Adriano (N)
Cafe Riggio (N&S)
Caffe Delle Stelle (N)
Caffe Greco (N&S)
Caffe Macaroni (S)
Caffe Roma (N&S)
Caffe Sport (S)
Capellini (N)
Capp's Corner (N)
Carrara's Cafe (N&S)
Casanova/S (N&S)
Castagnola's (N&S)
Ciao Ristorante (N)
Dal Baffo (N&S)
Eleven Rist. & Bar (N&S)
Emporio Armani (N)
Enrico's (N&S)
Ernesto's (N&S)
Fior D'Italia (N)
Gira Polli (N&S)
Gray Whale (N&S)
Grissini (N)
Hyde St. Bistro (N)
I Fratelli (N&S)
Il Fornaio (N)
Iron Horse (N)
Jackson Fillmore (S)
Kuleto's Italian (N)
Kuleto's Trattoria (N)
La Fiammetta (N)
Laghi (N)
La Ginestra (S)
La Pergola (N)
La Traviata (N&S)
Little Henry's (S)
Little Italy (S)
Little Joe's (N&S)
Marin Joe's (N&S)
Mario's Bohemian (N)
Mescolanza (N)
New Joe's (N&S)
North Beach (N&S)
Oliveto (N)
Original Joe's (N&S)
Oritalia (N&S)
Osteria (N)
Palermo/S (S)
Palio D'Asti (N)
Pane e Vino (N)
Paolo's/S (N&S)
Parma (N)
Pasta Moon/S (N&S)
Pasta Prego/N (N)
Pazzia Caffe (N&S)
Piatti/N (N)
Piazza D'Angelo (N&S)
Prego (N&S)
Rendezvous (N&S)
Restaurant Enoteca (N&S)
Rist. Ecco (N)
Rist. Fabrizio (N)
Rist. Lucca (N)
Rist. Milano (N)
Rosmarino (N&S)
Sardine Factory/S (N&S)
Spiedini (N)
Spuntino (N)
Stinking Rose (N&S)
Tarantino's (N&S)
Ti Bacio (N&S)
Tommaso's (S)
Tratt. Contadina (N&S)
Tra Vigne/N (N&S)
Tre Fratelli (N&S)
Tre Scalini/N (N)
Umberto (N)
U.S. Restaurant (N)
Vanessi's (N)
Venezia (N&S)
Venticello (N)
Vicolo Pizzeria (N&S)
Vince S.F. (N&S)
Vivande Porta Via (S)
Washington Sq. B & G (N)
Zza's Tratt. (N&S)

Japanese

Benihana
Cafe 222
Ebisu
Edokko
Elka
Goro's Robato
Iroha
Isobune Sushi
Kabuto Sushi

Kansai
Kirala
Kyo-Ya
Mifune
O Chame
Oritalia
Osome
Sanppo
Tanuki
Yamato
Yoshida-Ya
Yoshi's

Jewish

Brother's Deli*
Saul's Deli
(* Kosher)

Korean

Hahn's Hibachi
King Charcoal BBQ
Korea House
Seoul Garden

Mediterranean

Aqua
Bay Wolf
Cafe Chez Panisse
Chez Panisse
Faz
Garibaldi
Lalime's
La Mediterranee
Little City
LuLuBis/Cafe/Rest.
Palomino
Plump Jack Cafe
Rendezvous
Rivoli Restaurant
San Benito Hse./S
Splendido's
Square One
Zax
Zuni Cafe
Zza's Tratt.

Mexican

Alejandro's
Cactus Cafe
Cadillac Bar
Cafe Marimba
Campo Santo
Casa Aguila
Chevys
El Tapatio
Guaymas
La Cumbre
La Taqueria
Leticia's
Mom Is Cooking
Roosevelt Tamale
Taqueria Mission
Tortola
¡Wa-Ha-Ka!

Middle Eastern

La Mediterranee

Moroccan

Mamounia
Marrakech

Pacific Rim

Casa Madrona
Silks

Persian

Faz

Pizza

Basta Pasta
Bucci's
Cafe Chez Panisse
Cal. Pizza Kit.
Eleven Rist. & Bar
Gray Whale
Grissini
La Ginestra
Milano Pizzeria
Mozarella di Bufala
Olive's Pizza
Pauline's Pizza
Postrio
Ruby's
Tommaso's
Vicolo Pizzeria
Zachary's
Zza's Tratt.

Seafood

Adriatic
Alioto's
Aqua

A. Sabella's
Barnaby's By Bay
Caffe Sport
Castagnola's
Crow's Nest/S
Crustacean
Eastside Oyster/N
Ebisu
Elka
Gate Five
Gertie's
Gulf Coast G & B
Half Shell
Hayes St. Grill
Horizons
Maye's Hse.
McCormick/Kutelo
Orig. Old Clam Hse.
Pacific Cafe
Pacific Fresh/S
Pacific Heights
PJ's Oyster Bed
Sam's Anchor
Sam's Grill
Sardine Factory/S
Scoma's
Scott's Seafood
Spenger's Fish
Sunset Dining Rm./S
Swan Oyster Depot
Tadich Grill
Tarantino's
Waterfront, The
Yuet Lee

Singaporean
Straits Cafe

South American
Alejandro's

Southern
Blue Chalk Cafe
Catahoula/N
Doug's BBQ

Southwestern
Abiquiu
Cacti Grill
Santa Fe B & G
Tortola

Spanish
Alejandro's
Esperpento
Guernica
Iberia
Sol y Luna

Steakhouses
Alfred's
Crow's Nest/S
Eulipia/S
Harris'
House of Prime Rib
Izzy's Steak
Morton's
Vic Stewart's

Taiwanese
Taiwan

Thai
Dusit Thai
Khan Toke Thai
Manora's Thai
Marnee Thai
Narai
Plearn Thai
Royal Thai
Samui Thai
San Francisco BBQ
Siam Cuisine
Thep Phanom

Vegetarian
(Most Chinese, Indian and Thai restaurants)
Dottie's Cafe
Fleur de Lys
Greens
Island Cafe
Long Life Vegi Hse.
Sally's

Vietnamese
Aux Delices
Cordon Bleu
Emerald Garden
Golden Turtle
Kim's
Mai's
Tu Lan

NEIGHBORHOOD LOCATIONS

San Francisco

Castro/Noe
Bacco
Cafe Flore
Eric's Chinese
Firefly
La Mediterranee
Leticia's
Little Italy
Marnee Thai
South China Cafe

Chinatown
Empress of China
House of Nanking
Hunan Rest.
Imperial Palace
Lichee Garden
Yamato
Yuet Lee

Civic Center
Act IV
Bahia
Bistro Clovis
Caffe Delle Stelle
Cal. Cul. Academy
Geva's
Hayes St. Grill
Ivy's
Max's Opera Cafe
Spuntino
Stars
Stars Cafe
Suppenkuche
Vicolo Pizzeria
Vince S.F.
Zuni Cafe

Downtown
Abiquiu
Annabelle's
Anjou
Aqua
Bardelli's
Big Four
Bistro M
Bix
Brasserie Savoy
Cafe Akimbo
Cafe Bastille
Cafe Claude
Cafe Mozart
Cafe 222
Cal. Roastery
Cal. Pizza Kit.
Campton Place
Carnelian Room
Chambord
China Moon Cafe
Ciao Ristorante
City of Paris
Club 181
Cypress Club
Dottie's Cafe
Emporio Armani
Ernie's
Faz
Fleur de Lys
Fog City Diner
Garden Court
Harbor Village
Il Fornaio
India House
Iron Horse
Jack's
Julius' Castle
Kansai
Kelly's on Trinity
Kuleto's Italian
Kyo-Ya
La Scene
Le Central Bistro
Liberté
L'Olivier
London Wine Bar
MacArthur Park
Mama's
Marrakech
Masa's

Maxfield's B & G
Morton's
Narsai's Cafe
New Joe's
Occidental Grill
Original Joe's
Pacific
Palio D'Asti
Park Grill
Pier 23 Cafe
Postrio
Regina's
Rendezvous
Rist. Milano
Roti
Rotunda, The
Rubicon
Sam's Grill
Schroeder's
Scott's Seafood
Sears Fine Foods
Silks
Sol y Luna
Splendido's
Square One
Tadich Grill
Tommy Toy's
Tu Lan
Victor's
Yank Sing

East Bay

A La Carte
Alexander
Bay Wolf
Bette's Oceanview
Bridges
Bucci's
Cafe Chez Panisse
Cafe de Bordeaux
Cafe Fanny
Carrara's Cafe
Chevys
Chez Panisse
Citron
Doug's BBQ
Edokko
Fana Ethiopian
Fat Apple's
Gertie's
Ginger Island
Grissini
Gulf Coast G & B
Jade Villa
Kirala
Lalime's
La Mediterranee
Le Marquis
Long Life Vegi Hse.
Mama's Royal Cafe
Metropole
Nadine's
Nan Yang
O Chame
Oliveto
Omnivore
Pavilion
Plearn Thai
Restaurant Enoteca
Rivoli Restaurant
Rue de Main
Santa Fe B & G
Saul's Deli
Siam Cuisine
Spenger's Fish
Spiedini
Taiwan
Thornhill Cafe
Ti Bacio
Tourelle Cafe
Venezia
Vic Stewart's
Wente Bros.
Yoshi's
Yujean's
Zachary's
Zza's Tratt.

Haight-Ashbury

Cha Cha Cha's
Indian Oven
Thep Phanom

Japantown

Benihana
Elka
Iroha
Isobune Sushi

Korea House
Mifune
Sanppo
Seoul Garden

Mission
Dusit Thai
Esperpento
Flying Saucer
La Cumbre
La Taqueria
La Traviata
Le Trou
Manora's Thai
Mom Is Cooking
Orig. Old Clam Hse.
Pauline's Pizza
Roosevelt Tamale
Taqueria Mission
Ti Couz
Woodward's Garden

Nob Hill
Bella Voce
Fournou's Ovens
French Room
Hyde St. Bistro
Le Club
Nob Hill
Ritz-Carlton Din. Rm.
Ritz-Carlton Terr.
Vanessi's
Venticello

North Beach
Alfred's
Allegro
Amelio's
Basta Pasta
Bocce Cafe
Brandy Ho's
Buca Giovanni
Cafe Jacqueline
Caffe Greco
Caffe Macaroni
Caffe Roma
Caffe Sport
Campo Santo
Capp's Corner
Enrico's
Fior D'Italia
Gira Polli
Helmand
Little City
Little Joe's
Mama's
Mario's Bohemian
Moose's
Mo's Burgers
North Beach
Stinking Rose
Tommaso's
Tratt. Contadina
U.S. Restaurant
Washington Sq. B & G
Zax

Pacific Heights
Cafe Kati
Curbside Cafe
Elite Cafe, The
Garibaldi
Heights, The
Jackson Fillmore
Kim's
La Fiammetta
La Mediterranee
Mozarella di Bufala
Oritalia
Osome
Osteria
Pacific Heights
Pauli's Cafe
Rasselas
Sherman House
Tortola
Tre Fratelli
Trio Cafe
Vivande Porta Via

Palo Alto
Blue Chalk Cafe
Gaylord Indian
Gordon Biersch
Il Fornaio
L'Amie Donia
Osteria
Piatti
Scott's Seafood
Vicolo Pizzeria

Peninsula
Brother's Deli
Buffalo Grill
Cafe/All Seasons
Capellini
Dal Baffo
Flea St. Cafe
Flower Lounge
Iberia
Jin Jiang Kee Joon
JoAnn's B Street
JoAnn's Cafe
Kuleto's Trattoria
Stanford Park
231 Ellsworth

Potrero Hill
Asimakopoulos
Aux Delices
Sally's
San Francisco BBQ

Redwood City
Barbarossa
Bella Vista
Clark's by Bay

Richmond
Alain Rondelli
Alejandro's
Angkor Wat
Bill's Place
Cafe Maisonnette
Cafe Riggio
Cheer's Cafe
China House
Clement St. B & G
Cliff House
Courtyard B & G
Ebisu
Ernesto's
Flower Lounge
Fountain Court
Golden Turtle
Kabuto Sushi
Khan Toke Thai
King Charcoal BBQ
King of China
Kirin
La Bergerie
Laghi
Le Cyrano
Mai's
Mamounia
Mandalay
Mayflower
Mel's Drive-In
Mescolanza
Narai
Ocean Restaurant
Pacific Cafe
Pat O'Shea's
Rosmarino
Straits Cafe
Tanuki
Ton Kiang
Yet Wah

SOMA
Ace Cafe
Acorn Tea
Appam
Bizou
Boulevard
Cadillac Bar
Caribbean Zone
Cava 555
Chevys
Delancey St.
Eddie Rickenbacker's
Eleven Rist. & Bar
Embarko
ERIC Restaurant
Fly Trap
Fringale
Gordon Biersch
Half Shell
Hamburger Mary's
Harry Denton's
Julie's
Kiss
LuLuBis/Cafe/Rest.
Max's Diner
One Market
Palomino
Pazzia Caffe
Primo Patio Cafe
Rist. Ecco
Ruby's

South Park Cafe
Umberto
¡Wa-Ha-Ka!
Wu Kong

Sunset

Cafe/All Seasons
Casa Aguila
Milano Pizzeria
PJ's Oyster Bed

Union Street

Baker St. Bistro
Balboa Cafe
Blue Light
Bonta
Buchanan Grill
Cafe Adriano
Cafe Marimba
Doidge's
Greens
Izzy's Steak
La Pergola
L'Entrecote
Mel's Drive-In
North India
Olive's Pizza
Pane e Vino
Paragon
Parma
Perry's
Plump Jack Cafe
Prego
Samui Thai
Scott's Seafood
Yoshida-Ya

Van Ness/Polk

Acquerello
Adriatic
Aux Delices
Cafe Majestic
Cordon Bleu
Crustacean
Emerald Garden
Golden Turtle
Hahn's Hibachi
Hard Rock Cafe
Harris'
House of Prime Rib
I Fratelli
Johnny Love's
La Folie
Little Henry's
Maharani India
Maye's Hse.
Miss Pearl's Jam
Phnom Penh
Swan Oyster Depot
Tommy's Joynt
¡Wa-Ha-Ka!

Wharf

Alioto's
A. Sabella's
Castagnola's
Chez Michel
El Tapatio
Gaylord Indian
Mandarin, The
McCormick/Kutelo
Old Swiss House
Scoma's
Tarantino's
Waterfront, The
Yet Wah

BEYOND SAN FRANCISCO
North

Marin

Adriana's
Alta Mira
Avalon
Avenue Grill
Baci Caffe
Barnaby's By Bay
Buckeye Roadhse.
Cacti Grill
Cactus Cafe
California Cafe
Caprice, The
Casa Madrona
Chevys

El Paseo
Gate Five
Gira Polli
Goro's Robato
Gray Whale
Guaymas
Guernica
Horizons
Island Cafe
La Ginestra
La Petite Auberge
Lark Creek Inn
Left Bank
Mandarin House
Marin Joe's
North Sea Village
Pacific T & G
Panama Hotel
Piazza D'Angelo
Rice Table
Rist. Fabrizio
Rist. Lucca
Royal Thai
Sam's Anchor
Sand Dollar
Savannah Grill
Station House
Yet Wah

Mendocino
Cafe Beaujolais

Napa
Auberge du Soleil
Bistro D. Giovanni
Brava Terrace
Catahoula
Domaine Chandon
Foothill Cafe
French Laundry
Meadowood Rest.
Meadowood Grill
Mustards Grill
Napa Vall. Wine
Pasta Prego
Piatti
Showley's
Stars Oakville
Terra
Tra Vigne
Trilogy

Sonoma
Chateau Souverain
Downtown Bakery
Eastside Oyster
Grille
John Ash & Co.
Kenwood
Madrona Manor
Piatti
Samba Java
Tre Scalini

South

Half Moon Bay
Pasta Moon/S
San Benito Hse./S

Los Altos
Beausejour
Chef Chu's

Los Gatos
California Cafe
Los Gatos

Monterey/Carmel
Casanova
Central 159
Club XIX
Covey, The
Fresh Cream
Pacific's Edge
Rio Grill
Sardine Factory
Sierra Mar
Tarpy's Roadhouse

Mountain View
Chez T.J.

San Jose
Benihana
Campbell House
Emile's

Eulipia
Fung Lum
Gervais
Gordon Biersch
Il Fornaio
La Forêt
La Mère Michelle
Le Mouton Noir
Le Papillon
Lion & Compass
Pacific Fresh
Palermo
Paolo's
Plumed Horse

Santa Cruz

Chez Renee
Crow's Nest
Sunset Dining Rm.

Yosemite

Erna's House

SPECIAL FEATURES AND APPEALS

Breakfast
(All major hotels and the following standouts)
Barnaby's By Bay
Bette's Oceanview
Bill's Place
Brother's Deli
Cafe Claude
Cafe Fanny
Cafe Flore
Caffe Greco
Caffe Roma
Casa Aguila
Casanova/S
Castagnola's
Chambord
Cliff House
Curbside Cafe
Doidge's
Dottie's Cafe
Downtown Bakery/N
Elka
Fat Apple's
Gray Whale
Hamburger Mary's
La Mediterranee
Mama's
Mama's Royal Cafe
Mel's Drive-In
New Joe's
Original Joe's
Paolo's/S
Perry's
Roosevelt Tamale
Sally's
Samba Java/N
Saul's Deli
Sears Fine Foods
South Park Cafe
Spuntino
Stars
Station House
Taiwan
Thornhill Cafe
Trio Cafe
U.S. Restaurant
Yank Sing
Zuni Cafe
Zza's Tratt.

Brunch
(Best of many)
Acorn Tea
Balboa Cafe
Bette's Oceanview
Cafe Bastille
Cafe Beaujolais/N
Cafe/All Seasons
Cafe Majestic
Cafe Marimba
Clement St. B & G
Cliff House
Courtyard B & G
Curbside Cafe
Delancey St.
Elka
Flea St. Cafe
Fournou's Ovens
Hamburger Mary's
Horizons
Il Fornaio
Jackson Fillmore
L'Entrecote
Mama's Royal Cafe
Max's Diner
Meadowood Rest./N
Mel's Drive-In
Napa Vall. Wine/N
Park Grill
Pauli's Cafe
Postrio
Rosmarino
Sam's Anchor
Saul's Deli
Spuntino
Taiwan
Yank Sing
Zza's Tratt.

Buffet Served
(Check prices, days and times)
Cafe 222
Cal. Cul. Academy

Casa Madrona
Cliff House
Fana Ethiopian
French Room
Garden Court
Gaylord Indian
Gulf Coast G & B
Hunan Rest.
Kelly's on Trinity
Maharani India
Nob Hill
Pacific's Edge/S
Panama Hotel
Pavilion
Ritz-Carlton Terr.
Stanford Park
Sunset Dining Rm./S
Ti Bacio

Business Dining

Abiquiu
Aqua
Big Four
Boulevard
Carnelian Room
Chambord
Cypress Club
Ernie's
Fournou's Ovens
French Room
Harris'
Hayes St. Grill
House of Prime Rib
Il Fornaio
Iron Horse
Ivy's
Jack's
John Ash & Co./N
Kuleto's Italian
La Folie
La Mère Michelle/S
Le Central Bistro
Le Club
Liberté
Lion & Compass/S
L'Olivier
LuLuBis/Cafe/Rest.
MacArthur Park
Mandarin, The
Masa's
McCormick/Kuleto
Moose's
One Market
Park Grill
Postrio
Ritz-Carlton Din. Rm.
Rubicon
Sherman House
Silks
Sol y Luna
Square One
Stars
Tadich Grill
231 Ellsworth
Umberto
Zuni Cafe

BYO

Eastside Oyster/N
Mandarin, The
Nob Hill
Rio Grill/S

Caters

(Some of the many, in addition to hotel restaurants)

Acquerello
Act IV
Angkor Wat
Appam
Aqua
Asimakopoulos
Bahia
Barnaby's By Bay
Beausejour/S
Big Four
Blue Light
Brava Terrace/N
Brother's Deli
Buffalo Grill
Cadillac Bar
Cafe Claude
Cafe Jacqueline
Cafe Kati
Cafe Marimba
Cafe 222
Caffe Macaroni

Caffe Roma
California Cafe/N
Cal. Roastery
Cal. Pizza Kit.
Campo Santo
Casa Aguila
Casanova/S
Castagnola's
Central 159/S
Chambord
Cheer's Cafe
Chef Chu's/S
Chevys
China Moon Cafe
Ciao Ristorante
Clark's By Bay
Club 181
Curbside Cafe
Dal Baffo
Dottie's Cafe
Doug's BBQ
Downtown Bakery/N
Eastside Oyster/N
Ebisu
Emile's/S
Emporio Armani
Empress of China
ERIC Restaurant
Fana Ethiopian
Flea St. Cafe
Fleur de Lys
Flying Saucer
Fly Trap
Fountain Court
Fung Lum/S
Garibaldi
Gaylord Indian
Gertie's
Gervais/S
Geva's
Gira Polli
Gordon Biersch
Goro's Robato
Gray Whale
Guaymas
Gulf Coast G & B
Half Shell
Hard Rock Cafe
Horizons
Hyde St. Bistro
Iberia
Imperial Palace
Indian Oven
Island Cafe
Isobune Sushi
Izzy's Steak
Jade Villa
Jin Jiang Kee Joon
JoAnn's B Street
JoAnn's Cafe
John Ash & Co./N
Johnny Love's
Julie's
Kansai
Kelly's on Trinity
Kirin
Korea House
La Bergerie
La Fiammetta
La Folie
Lalime's
La Mediterranee
La Pergola
La Petite Auberge
Le Club
Le Marquis
Le Mouton Noir/S
L'Entrecote
Le Papillon/S
Leticia's
Le Trou
Liberté
Little Henry's
London Wine Bar
MacArthur Park
Maharani India
Mama's Royal Cafe
Mandarin, The
Maye's Hse.
Mescolanza
Milano Pizzeria
Miss Pearl's Jam
Mom Is Cooking
Mustards Grill/N
Narsai's Cafe
New Joe's

North India
Ocean Restaurant
O Chame
Olive's Pizza
One Market
Original Joe's
Osome
Pacific Fresh/S
Pacific Heights
Palermo/S
Palio D'Asti
Paolo's/S
Pasta Moon/S
Pauli's Cafe
Perry's
Piazza D'Angelo
Plearn Thai
Postrio
Rasselas
Rendezvous
Rio Grill/S
Rist. Ecco
Royal Thai
Ruby's
Rue de Main
Sally's
Samba Java/N
San Benito Hse./S
San Francisco BBQ
Santa Fe B & G
Saul's Deli
Schroeder's
Scott's Seafood
Siam Cuisine
Sol y Luna
Spuntino
Stanford Park
Straits Cafe
Sunset Dining Rm./S
Tarpy's Roadhouse/S
Ti Bacio
Vic Stewart's
Vivande Porta Via
Yank Sing
Yet Wah
Yoshida-Ya
Yuet Lee
Yujean's
Zza's Tratt.

Dancing/Entertainment

(Check days, times and performers for entertainment; D = dancing)

Ace Cafe (jazz)
Act IV (piano)
A La Carte (jazz)
Alejandro's (guitar)
Alexander (piano)
Angkor Wat (trad. dance)
A. Sabella's (piano)
Asimakopoulos (fortune teller)
Avalon (Hawaiian/jazz)
Bahia (bossa nova)
Beausejour/S (piano)
Bella Voce (piano/opera)
Big Four (piano)
Bix (jazz trio)
Cadillac Bar (varies)
Cafe Bastille (jazz)
Cafe Claude (jazz)
Cafe Majestic (piano)
Cafe Marimba (mariachi)
California Cafe/N (piano)
Caribbean Zone (D/Caribbean)
Casa Madrona (piano)
Cava 555 (jazz)
Chambord (jazz)
Cliff House (piano)
Club 181 (jazz)
Covey, The/S (piano)
Crow's Nest/S (D/varies)
Emporio Armani (jazz)
Enrico's (jazz)
Esperpento (music)
Fly Trap (jazz)
Garden Court (harpist)
Gate Five (guitar)
Grille/N (piano)
Gulf Coast G & B (jazz)
Hard Rock Cafe (band)
Harris' (jazz/piano/bass)
Harry Denton's (blues)
Hunan Rest. (D)
Jade Villa (D)
Johnny Love's (D/band)
Julie's (D/soul/r&b)
Khan Toke Thai (Thai dancer)

La Scene (jazz/piano)
L'Entrecote (D/band)
Mamounia (belly dancer)
Marin Joe's (piano)
Marrakech (belly dancer)
Maxfield's B & G (band)
Max's Opera Cafe (singing staff)
Maye's Hse. (piano/singer)
Metropole (jazz)
Miss Pearl's Jam (D/varies)
Moose's (jazz)
Napa Vall. Wine/N (guitar/violin)
O Chame (band)
Oliveto (flamenco)
Pacific's Edge/S (piano/jazz)
Panama Hotel (jazz)
Paragon (band)
Pauline's Pizza (band)
Pavilion (piano/violin)
Pier 23 Cafe (D/varies)
Plumed Horse/S (D/band)
Rasselas (D/jazz/blues)
Regina's (jazz)
Rendezvous (jazz)
Ritz-Carlton Din. Rm. (jazz/harp)
Ritz-Carlton Terr. (jazz trio)
Santa Fe B & G (piano)
Saul's Deli (Jewish)
Sherman House (piano)
Showley's/N (jazz trio)
Silks (piano)
Sol y Luna (Latin)
Station House (jazz)
Tarpy's Roadhouse/S (jazz)
Tourelle Cafe (jazz)
Umberto (piano)
Vanessi's (piano)
Vic Stewart's (varies)
Vince S.F. (jazz)
Wente Bros. (concert series)
Zuni Cafe (piano)

Delivers*/Takeout

(Nearly all Asians, coffee shops, delis, diners & pasta/pizzerias deliver or do takeout; here are some interesting possibilities; D = delivery, T = takeout)

Ace Cafe (T)
Acorn Tea (T)
Adriana's/N (T)
Adriatic (T)
A La Carte (T)
Alexander (T)
Alfred's (T)
Amelio's (D)
Anjou (T)
Aqua (T)
Auberge du Soleil/N (T)
Avenue Grill (T)
Baci Caffe (D,T)
Balboa Cafe (T)
Bardelli's (D,T)
Beausejour/S (T)
Bella Vista (T)
Bizou (T)
Blue Light (T)
Bonta (T)
Brava Terrace/N (T)
Buchanan Grill (T)
Buffalo Grill (T)
Cacti Grill (T)
Cafe Adriano (T)
Cafe Akimbo (T)
Cafe Beaujolais/N (T)
Cafe Claude (T)
Cafe de Bordeaux (D,T)
Cafe Fanny (T)
Cafe Flore (T)
Cafe Kati (T)
Cafe Marimba (D,T)
Cafe Riggio (T)
Caffe Delle Stelle (T)
Caffe Greco (T)
Caffe Macaroni (T)
Caffe Roma (D,T)
Caffe Sport (T)
Cal. Cul. Academy (T)
California Cafe/N (T)
Cal. Roastery (D,T)
Campo Santo (T)
Capellini (T)
Capp's Corner (D,T)
Carnelian Room (T)
Carrara's Cafe (T)
Casa Aguila (T)
Casanova/S (T)
Castagnola's (T)
Cava 555 (T)

Central 159/S (T)
Cha Cha Cha's (T)
Chambord (T)
Cheer's Cafe (T)
Chevys (T)
Ciao Ristorante (T)
City of Paris (T)
Clark's By Bay (T)
Clement St. B & G (T)
Courtyard B & G (T)
Curbside Cafe (T)
Dal Baffo (T)
Doidge's (T)
Downtown Bakery/N (T)
Eastside Oyster/N (T)
Embarko (T)
Ernesto's (T)
Fior D'Italia (T)
Flea St. Cafe (D,T)
Fly Trap (D,T)
Fog City Diner (T)
Foothill Cafe/N (T)
Fournou's Ovens (T)
French Room (T)
Fringale (T)
Garibaldi (D,T)
Gate Five (T)
Gertie's (T)
Gira Polli (D,T)
Gray Whale (T)
Half Shell (D,T)
Hamburger Mary's (T)
Hard Rock Cafe (T)
Harry Denton's (T)
Horizons (T)
House of Prime Rib (T)
Hyde St. Bistro (T)
Il Fornaio (T)
Iron Horse (T)
Island Cafe (D,T)
Ivy's (T)
Izzy's Steak (T)
Johnny Love's (T)
Julie's (T)
Kelly's on Trinity (D,T)
Kiss (T)
La Bergerie (D,T)
La Fiammetta (T)
Laghi (T)
La Ginestra (T)
La Mère Michelle/S (T)
La Pergola (T)
La Petite Auberge (D,T)
Le Central Bistro (T)
L'Entrecote (T)
Little Henry's (T)
Little Italy (T)
Little Joe's (T)
L'Olivier (D,T)
London Wine Bar (D,T)
Los Gatos/S (T)
LuLuBis/Cafe/Rest. (T)
MacArthur Park (T)
Marin Joe's (T)
Mario's Bohemian (T)
Mescolanza (T)
Mo's Burgers (T)
Mustards Grill/N (T)
Narsai's Cafe (D,T)
New Joe's (T)
North Beach (T)
One Market (D)
Original Joe's (D,T)
Orig. Old Clam Hse. (T)
Oritalia (T)
Osteria (T)
Pacific Fresh/S (T)
Pacific Heights (T)
Pacific's Edge/S (T)
Palio D'Asti (T)
Palomino (T)
Panama Hotel (T)
Pane e Vino (T)
Paolo's/S (T)
Park Grill (D,T)
Pasta Prego/N (T)
Pauli's Cafe (T)
Perry's (T)
Piatti/N (T)
Piazza D'Angelo (T)
Plumed Horse/S (T)
Plump Jack Cafe (T)
Prego (T)
Rendezvous (T)
Restaurant Enoteca (T)
Rio Grill/S (T)
Rist. Ecco (T)
Rist. Fabrizio (T)

Rist. Lucca (T)
Rist. Milano (T)
Ritz-Carlton Din. Rm. (T)
Ritz-Carlton Terr. (T)
Rosmarino (T)
Ruby's (D,T)
Rue de Main (T)
Samba Java/N (T)
Sand Dollar (T)
Sardine Factory/S (D,T)
Savannah Grill (T)
Schroeder's (T)
Scott's Seafood (T)
Sears Fine Foods (T)
South Park Cafe (T)
Splendido's (T)
Spuntino (T)
Square One (T)
Stanford Park (T)
Station House (T)
Stinking Rose (T)
Suppenkuche (T)
Tadich Grill (T)
Tarpy's Roadhouse/S (D,T)
Thornhill Cafe (T)
Ti Bacio (T)
Tommy's Joynt (T)
Tratt. Contadina (T)
Tra Vigne/N (T)
Trio Cafe (T)
U.S. Restaurant (T)
Vanessi's (D,T)
Venezia (T)
Vince S.F. (T)
Vivande Porta Via (D,T)
Washington Sq. B & G (T)
Waterfront, The (D,T)
Yuet Lee (T)
(*Call to check range and charges, if any)

Dining Alone

(Other than hotels, coffeehouses, sushi bars and counter service places)
House of Nanking
JoAnn's B Street
La Mère Michelle/S
South Park Cafe
Umberto
Vanessi's

Fireplaces

A La Carte
Alta Mira
Amelio's
A. Sabella's
Auberge du Soleil/N
Avalon
Bella Vista
Big Four
Blue Chalk Cafe
Brava Terrace/N
Brother's Deli
Buckeye Roadhse.
Cafe Mozart
California Cafe/N
Campbell House/S
Caprice, The
Casa Madrona
Chambord
Chateau Souverain/N
Chez Renee/S
Chez T.J.
Clark's By Bay
Clement St. B & G
Covey, The/S
Crow's Nest/S
Domaine Chandon/N
Eastside Oyster/N
El Paseo
El Tapatio
Erna's House/S
French Laundry/N
Gate Five
Guaymas
House of Prime Rib
Iberia
John Ash & Co./N
Kenwood/N
Kuleto's Italian
Lark Creek Inn
Le Mouton Noir/S
Liberté
Los Gatos/S
LuLuBis/Cafe/Rest.
Marin Joe's
Meadowood Rest./N

Metropole
Old Swiss House
Palermo/S
Paragon
Pasta Moon/S
Piazza D'Angelo
Plearn Thai
Plumed Horse/S
Rio Grill/S
Rist. Lucca
Roti
Sand Dollar
Sardine Factory/S
Sherman House
Stanford Park
Station House
Tarpy's Roadhouse/S
Tourelle Cafe
Vic Stewart's
Zuni Cafe

Game in Season
(The following are recommended)
Acquerello
Bix
Caribbean Zone
Ernie's
Hyde St. Bistro
I Fratelli
Iron Horse
Lark Creek Inn
Meadowood Rest./N
Stars

Health/Spa Menus
(Most places cook to order to meet any dietary request; call in advance to check; see also Health Food, Chinese, Indian and Thai; the following are good bets)
Catahoula/N
Covey, The/S
French Room
Grille/N
Island Cafe
Lark Creek Inn
Masa's
Max's Diner
Meadowood Rest./N
One Market
Paolo's/S
Pavilion
Sierra Mar/S
Square One
Station House
Ti Bacio

Historic Interest
(Year opened)
1861 Orig. Old Clam Hse.
1867 Maye's Hse.
1868 Garden Court*
1876 Sherman House*
1876 Woodward's Garden*
1884 Terra/N*
1886 Fior D'Italia*
1905 San Benito Hse./S*
1909 Bardelli's*
1909 Rotunda, The*
1912 Swan Oyster Depot
1915 Pavilion*
1920 A. Sabella's*
1920 Sam's Anchor
1926 Amelio's*
1926 Panama Hotel
1927 Bella Vista
1928 Alfred's*
1928 Alioto's*
1934 Ernie's
1937 Original Joe's
1949 Tadich Grill
(*Building)

Hotel Dining
Alta Mira Hotel
  Alta Mira
Auberge du Soleil
  Auberge du Soleil/N
Campton Place Hotel
  Campton Place
Claremont Resort & Spa
  Pavilion
Concord Hilton Hotel
  Grissini
Eldorado Hotel
  Piatti/N

Fairmont Hotel
  Bella Voce
Four Seasons Clift Hotel
  French Room
Garden Court Hotel
  Il Fornaio
Harbor Court Hotel
  Harry Denton's
Highlands Inn
  Pacific's Edge/S
Hotel Griffon
  Roti
Hotel Majestic
  Cafe Majestic
Hotel Milano
  Bistro M
Hotel Nikko
  Cafe 222
Huntington Hotel
  Big Four
Inn at the Opera
  Act IV
Lodge at Pebble Beach
  Club XIX/S
Madrona Manor
  Madrona Manor/N
Mandarin Oriental Hotel
  Silks
Mark Hopkins Inter-Continental
  Nob Hill
Meadowood Resort
  Meadowood Grill/N
  Meadowood Rest./N
Miyako Hotel
  Elka
Mount View Hotel
  Catahoula/N
Oyster Point Marina Inn
  Pasta Moon/S
Panama Hotel
  Panama Hotel
Pan Pacific Hotel
  Pacfic Grill
Park Hyatt Hotel
  Park Grill
Post Ranch Inn
  Sierra Mar/S
Prescott Hotel
  Postrio
Quail Lodge Resort & Golf Club
  Covey, The/S
Raphael Hotel
  Mama's
Ritz-Carlton Hotel
  Dining Room
  Terrace
Savoy Hotel
  Brasserie Savoy
Shannon Court Hotel
  City of Paris
Sheraton Palace Hotel
  Garden Court
  Kyo-Ya
  Maxfield's B & G
Sherman House
  Sherman House
Sonoma Mission Inn
  Grille/N
Stanford Court Hotel
  Fournou's Ovens
Stanford Park Hotel
  Stanford Park
Villa Florence Hotel
  Kuleto's Italian
Warwick Regis Hotel
  La Scene Cafe
Westin St. Francis Hotel
  Victor's

"In" Places

Abiquiu
Ace Cafe
Acorn Tea
Acquerello
Alain Rondelli
Appam
Aqua
Avalon
Bahia
Balboa Cafe
Bette's Oceanview
Big Four
Bix
Blue Light
Boulevard
Brava Terrace/N
Bridges
Buckeye Roadhse.

Cafe Chez Panisse
Cafe Marimba
Caribbean Zone
Cava 555
Chez Panisse
Chez T.J.
Club 181
Cypress Club
Eleven Rist. & Bar
Elite Cafe, The
Elka
Embarko
Enrico's
Firefly
Fleur de Lys
Flying Saucer
Fog City Diner
Fringale
Harry Denton's
House of Nanking
Julie's
La Mère Michelle/S
Lark Creek Inn
Liberté
LuLuBis/Cafe/Rest.
Moose's
Mustards Grill/N
One Market
Paragon
Perry's
Plump Jack Cafe
Postrio
Rubicon
South Park Cafe
Square One
Stars Cafe
Tra Vigne/N
Tre Fratelli
Washington Sq. B & G
Zuni Cafe

Jacket Required

Alexander
Carnelian Room
Covey, The/S
Dal Baffo
Delancey St.
Ernie's
French Room
Garden Court
Julius' Castle
Lichee Garden
Masa's
One Market
Pacific's Edge/S
Plearn Thai
Ritz-Carlton Din. Rm.
Silks
Tommy Toy's
Tre Scalini/N
Victor's

Late Late – After 12:30

(All hours are AM)
Ace Cafe (12:45)
Avalon (2:30)
Basta Pasta (1:45)
Hamburger Mary's (1:15)
King Charcoal BBQ (3)
Korea House (1)
Mama's (2)
Original Joe's (1)
Park Grill (24 hrs.)
Regina's (1)
Sherman House (24 hrs.)
Tommy's Joynt (2)
¡Wa-Ha-Ka! (1)
Yuet Lee (3)

Meet for a Drink

(Most top hotels and the following standouts)
Bix
Blue Light
Buchanan Grill
Buckeye Roadhse.
Caribbean Zone
Cliff House
Cypress Club
Eleven Rist. & Bar
Gordon Biersch
Guaymas
Hamburger Mary's
Hard Rock Cafe
Harry Denton's
Johnny Love's
London Wine Bar
Moose's
Mustards Grill/N

North Beach
One Market
Paragon
Perry's
Prego
Postrio
Stars
Tosca Cafe*
Tra Vigne/N
Washington Sq. B & G
Zuni Cafe
(*Not included in *Survey*)

Noteworthy Newcomers (44)

Abiquiu
Anjou
Avalon
Bacco
Bistro M
Blue Chalk Cafe
Buffalo Grill
Cafe Adriano
Cafe Akimbo
Catahoula/N
Chez Michel
Citron
Club 181
Eleven Rist. & Bar
ERIC Restaurant
Esperpento
Faz
Firefly
Foothill Cafe/N
Gate Five
Heights, The
Kiss
L'Amie Donia
Left Bank
Liberté
Lichee Garden
Los Gatos/S
Morton's
Occidental Grill
Pacific
Palomino
Paragon
Pazzia Caffe
Piazza D'Angelo
Plump Jack Cafe
Primo Patio Cafe
Regina's
Rivoli Restaurant
Rubicon
Stars Oakville/N
Suppenkuche
Ti Couz
Vic Stewart's
Zax

Noteworthy Closings (46)

Alessia
Bentley's
Cafe Fontebella
Cafe Justin
Cairo Cafe
Casablanca
Celadon
Circolo
Citrus N. African Grill
Corona Bar & Grill
DePaula's Brazilian
Diamond Street
Donatello
Etrusca
Fillmore Grill
Franco's
Geordy's
Giramonti
Giuliano's
Himalaya Rest. & Sweets
Hong Kong Tea House
Ichiban-Kan
Ironwood Cafe
Jesters
Kan's
La Roca Restaurant
La Rocca's Oyster Bar
Lascaux
Le Castel
Le Domino
L'Escargot
Milano Joe's
Medioevo
Modella Ristorante
Modesto Lanzone
Nadine's
Pacific Grill

Piemonte Ovest
Pietro's
Pixley Cafe
Remillards
Riera's
Rist. Grifone
Squid's Cafe
Suzie Kate's
Truffles

Offbeat

Ace Cafe
Acorn Tea
Bahia
Caffe Sport
Campo Santo
Caribbean Zone
Cha Cha Cha's
China Moon Cafe
Club 181
Cypress Club
Delancey St.
Dottie's Cafe
Esperpento
Flying Saucer
Geva's
Hamburger Mary's
Helmand
Indian Oven
Mamounia
Mario's Bohemian
Marrakech
Miss Pearl's Jam
Panama Hotel
Pauline's Pizza
Pier 23 Cafe
Straits Cafe
Ti Couz
Tommy's Joynt
U.S. Restaurant

Outdoor Dining

(Best of many)
Acorn Tea
Adriana's/N
Alta Mira
Appam
Auberge du Soleil/N
Baker St. Bistro
Barnaby's By Bay
Basta Pasta
Bay Wolf
Bill's Place
Blue Chalk Cafe
Bocce Cafe
Brava Terrace/N
Bridges
Bucci's
Buckeye Roadhse.
Buffalo Grill
Cacti Grill
Cafe Bastille
Cafe Claude
Cafe Fanny
Cafe Flore
Caffe Greco
Caffe Roma
California Cafe/N
Casa Madrona
Catahoula/N
Chateau Souverain/N
Cheer's Cafe
Chevys
Chez Renee/S
Chez T.J.
Citron
Club XIX/S
Crow's Nest/S
Curbside Cafe
Delancey St.
Domaine Chandon/N
Eastside Oyster/N
El Paseo
Embarko
Emporio Armani
Enrico's
Erna's House/S
Flea St. Cafe
Fog City Diner
French Laundry/N
Gertie's
Geva's
Ginger Island
Gray Whale
Grille/N
Grissini
Guaymas
Hahn's Hibachi
Half Shell

Harry Denton's
Horizons
Hyde St. Bistro
Iberia
Il Fornaio
Island Cafe
John Ash & Co./N
Kelly's on Trinity
Kenwood/N
La Mère Michelle/S
La Taqueria
Lark Creek Inn
Le Mouton Noir/S
L'Entrecote
Lion & Compass/S
MacArthur Park
Madrona Manor/N
Meadowood Rest./N
Mel's Drive-In
Miss Pearl's Jam
Mom Is Cooking
O Chame
Oliveto
Pacific Fresh/S
Pacific T & G
Palermo/S
Palomino
Panama Hotel
Paolo's/S
Pasta Moon/S
Pasta Prego/N
Perry's
Piatti/N
Piazza D'Angelo
Pier 23 Cafe
Rendezvous
Rist. Fabrizio
Ritz-Carlton Terr.
Rosmarino
Roti
Royal Thai
Sally's
Sam's Anchor
San Benito Hse./S
Sand Dollar
Santa Fe B & G
Savannah Grill
Showley's/N
Sierra Mar/S
Sol y Luna
South Park Cafe
Spiedini
Splendido's
Square One
Stanford Park
Stars Oakville/N
Stinking Rose
Sunset Dining Rm./S
Thornhill Cafe
Ti Bacio
Tourelle Cafe
Trilogy/N
Trio Cafe
Umberto
Vince S.F.
Wente Bros.
Wu Kong
Zuni Cafe
Zza's Tratt.

Parking/Valet

(L = parking lot; V = valet parking; * = validated parking)

Abiquiu (V)
Acquerello (L)
Act IV (V)*
Adriana's/N (L)
Adriatic*
Alfred's (L,V)
Alioto's (V)*
Allegro*
Alta Mira (L,V)
Amelio's (V)*
Aqua (V)
A. Sabella's*
Auberge du Soleil/N (L,V)
Avalon*
Avenue Grill (L)
Baci Caffe (L)
Barbarossa (L)
Barnaby's By Bay (L)
Basta Pasta (V)*
Beausejour/S (L)
Bella Vista (L)
Bella Voce*
Big Four (V)
Bill's Place (L)
Bistro D. Giovanni/N (L)

Bix (V)
Bocce Cafe (V)
Boulevard (V)
Brasserie Savoy (V)
Brava Terrace/N (L)
Bridges (V)
Brother's Deli (L)
Bucci's (L)
Buckeye Roadhse. (L,V)
Buffalo Grill (L)
Cafe Claude (L)
Cafe Fanny (L)
Cafe Flore (L)
Cafe Kati*
Cafe Maisonnette (L)
Cafe Majestic (V)
Cafe 222*
Cal. Cul. Academy (L)
California Cafe/N (L)
Campbell House/S (L)
Campo Santo*
Campton Place (L,V)
Capellini (V)
Caprice, The (L,V)
Carnelian Room (L)
Casa Madrona (V)
Castagnola's (V)*
Central 159/S (L)
Cha Cha Cha's (L)
Chambord*
Chateau Souverain/N (L)
Chevys*
Chez Renee/S
China Moon Cafe (L)
Ciao Ristorante (V)*
City of Paris (L,V)
Clark's By Bay (L)
Cliff House (L)
Club 181*
Club XIX/S (V)
Courtyard B & G*
Covey, The/S (L)
Crow's Nest/S*
Crustacean (V)
Cypress Club (V)
Dal Baffo (L)
Delancey St. (V)
Domaine Chandon/N (L)
Edokko (L)
Eleven Rist. & Bar*
Elite Cafe, The (L)
Emile's/S (V)
Emporio Armani (V)
Emerald Garden*
Enrico's*
ERIC Restaurant (V)*
Erna's House/S (L)
Ernesto's (L)
Ernie's (V)*
Esperpento (L)
Eulipia/S*
Fat Apple's (L)
Fior D'Italia (V)
Flea St. Cafe (L)
Fleur de Lys (V)
Flower Lounge (L)
Fly Trap (V)*
Foothill Cafe/N (L)
Fournou's Ovens (V)*
French Room (V)
Fresh Cream/S*
Garden Court*
Garibaldi (V)
Gate Five (L)
Gaylord Indian (L)*
Gertie's*
Gervais/S (L)
Ginger Island (L)
Golden Turtle (V)*
Goro's Robato (L)
Gray Whale (L)
Greens (L)
Grille/N (L,V)
Grissini (L)
Guaymas*
Guernica (L)
Gulf Coast G & B (L)
Half Shell (L)
Hamburger Mary's*
Harbor Village (V)*
Hard Rock Cafe (V)
Harris' (V)
Harry Denton's (V)
Helmand*
Horizons (L,V)
House of Prime Rib (V)*
Hyde St. Bistro (V)
Iberia (L)

I Fratelli (V)
Il Fornaio (V)
India House (V)
Iroha*
Island Cafe (L)
Isobune Sushi*
Izzy's Steak*
Jack's (L)
Jin Jiang Kee Joon (L)
JoAnn's Cafe (V)
John Ash & Co./N (L)
Johnny Love's (V)
Julie's (L)
Julius' Castle (V)
Kansai (V)
Kelly's on Trinity (L)
Kenwood/N (L)
Kirala (L)
Kiss (L)
Korea House*
Kuleto's Trattoria (V)
Kyo-Ya (V)
La Folie (V)
La Forêt/S (L)
La Mère Michelle/S (L)
Lark Creek Inn (L)
La Scene (V)
La Traviata (V)
Le Club (V)
Le Cyrano (L)
Le Marquis (L)
Le Mouton Noir/S (L)
L'Entrecote (V)
Le Papillon/S (L)
Leticia's (L)
Liberté (L)
Lion & Compass/S (V)
Little Joe's (L)
L'Olivier (V)
Los Gatos/S (L)
LuLuBis/Cafe/Rest. (L)
MacArthur Park (V)
Madrona Manor/N (L)
Maharani India (V)*
Mandarin House (L)
Mandarin, The*
Marin Joe's (L,V)
Marrakech*
Masa's (V)
Maxfield's B & G (V)
Max's Opera Cafe (L)
Maye's Hse. (V)*
McCormick/Kutelo*
Meadowood Rest./N (L)
Mel's Drive-In (L)
Mescolanza (L)
Mifune (L)
Miss Pearl's Jam (V)
Moose's (V)
Mustards Grill/N (L)
Napa Vall. Wine/N (L)
Narsai's Cafe (L)
Nob Hill (L,V)*
North Beach (V)
North India (L)
Ocean Restaurant (L)
O Chame (L)
Old Swiss House*
Oliveto (L)
One Market (V)
Original Joe's (L,V)
Pacific Fresh/S (L)
Pacific T & G (L)
Pacific's Edge/S (V)
Palermo/S (L)
Palio D'Asti (V)
Palomino*
Pane e Vino*
Paolo's/S (L)*
Park Grill (L,V)*
Pasta Moon/S (L)
Pasta Prego/N (L)
Pavilion (L)
Piatti/N (L)
Piazza D'Angelo (V)
Pier 23 Cafe (L)
Plumed Horse/S (V)
Postrio (V)*
Regina's (V)
Rio Grill/S (L)
Rist. Fabrizio (L)*
Rist. Milano (L)
Ritz-Carlton Din. Rm. (L)
Ritz-Carlton Terr. (L)
Roti (V)
Royal Thai (L)

Rubicon (V)
Rue de Main*
Sally's (L)
Sanppo*
Santa Fe B & G (L,V)
Sardine Factory/S (L,V)
Savannah Grill (L)
Scoma's (V)
Seoul Garden*
Sherman House (V)
Silks (V)
Sol y Luna*
Spiedini (V)*
Splendido's*
Square One (V)
Stanford Park (L)
Stars Cafe (V)
Stars Oakville/N (L)
Station House (L)
Sunset Dining Rm./S (L,V)
Taiwan*
Tarantino's*
Tarpy's Roadhouse/S (L)
French Laundry/N (L)
Tommy Toy's (V)
Tommy's Joynt (L)
Ton Kiang (L)
Tourelle Cafe (V)*
Tra Vigne/N (L)
Tu Lan (L)
Umberto (V)
Vanessi's (L)*
Venezia (L)
Venticello (V)
Vic Stewart's (L)
Victor's (L,V)
Vince S.F. (L)
¡Wa-Ha-Ka! (V)
Washington Sq. B & G (V)*
Waterfront, The (V)
Wente Bros. (L,V)
Wu Kong*
Yet Wah*
Yoshida-Ya*
Yoshi's (L)
Zax*

Parties & Private Rooms

(Any nightclub or restaurant charges less at off-times; * indicates private rooms available; best of many)

Ace Cafe
Acorn Tea*
Adriatic
A La Carte*
Alain Rondelli
Alejandro's*
Alexander
Alfred's*
Alioto's *
Alta Mira*
Amelio's*
Angkor Wat
Anjou
Appam*
Aqua*
A. Sabella's*
Asimakopoulos
Auberge du Soleil/N*
Avalon
Avenue Grill*
Bacco
Bahia
Balboa Cafe
Bardelli's*
Barnaby's By Bay
Basta Pasta*
Beausejour/S*
Bella Vista*
Bella Voce*
Benihana
Big Four*
Bill's Place
Blue Chalk Cafe
Blue Light
Bocce Cafe
Boulevard*
Brandy Ho's*
Brasserie Savoy*
Brava Terrace/N*
Bridges
Brother's Deli*
Buchanan Grill*
Buckeye Roadhse.*
Buffalo Grill*

Cadillac Bar*
Cafe Adriano
Cafe Chez Panisse
Cafe Bastille*
Cafe Beaujolais/N
Cafe Claude*
Cafe de Bordeaux
Cafe Flore
Cafe Jacqueline
Cafe Kati*
Cafe Maisonnette
Cafe Majestic*
Cafe Mozart*
Cafe 222*
Caffe Macaroni*
Cal. Cul. Academy*
California Cafe/N*
Cal. Roastery
Campbell House/S*
Campo Santo
Campton Place*
Capellini*
Caribbean Zone
Carnelian Room*
Carrara's Cafe*
Casa Madrona*
Casanova/S*
Castagnola's*
Catahoula/N*
Cava 555
Central 159/S*
Chambord*
Chateau Souverain/N
Chef Chu's/S*
Chez Panisse
Chez Renee/S
Chez T.J.*
China House
Ciao Ristorante
Citron
City of Paris
Clark's By Bay*
Cliff House*
Club 181 *
Club XIX/S
Covey, The/S*
Crow's Nest/S*
Cypress Club*
Dal Baffo*
Delancey St.*
Domaine Chandon/N
Dusit Thai
Eastside Oyster/N*
Ebisu*
Edokko*
Eleven Rist. & Bar*
Elka*
El Paseo*
El Tapatio*
Embarko
Emerald Garden
Emile's/S*
Emporio Armani*
Empress of China*
ERIC Restaurant
Eric's Chinese
Erna's House/S*
Ernesto's
Ernie's*
Esperpento*
Eulipia/S
Fior D'Italia*
Firefly
Flea St. Cafe*
Fleur de Lys*
Flower Lounge*
Fly Trap*
Fog City Diner
Foothill Cafe/N
Fountain Court*
Fournou's Ovens*
French Laundry/N*
French Room
Fresh Cream/S*
Fung Lum/S*
Garden Court*
Garibaldi
Gate Five
Gaylord Indian*
Gertie's*
Gervais/S*
Ginger Island
Golden Turtle
Gordon Biersch
Goro's Robato
Gray Whale
Greens
Grille/N*

Grissini*
Guaymas*
Guernica*
Gulf Coast G & B*
Hahn's Hibachi
Half Shell*
Harbor Village*
Harris'*
Harry Denton's*
Hayes St. Grill
Horizons
Hunan Rest.*
Iberia*
Imperial Palace*
Iron Horse*
Island Cafe
Ivy's*
Izzy's Steak*
Jack's*
Jackson Fillmore
Jade Villa*
Jin Jiang Kee Joon*
Johnny Love's
Julie's*
Julius' Castle*
Kabuto Sushi*
Kansai*
Kelly's on Trinity*
Kenwood/N*
King Charcoal BBQ
Kirin
Kiss
Kuleto's Italian*
Kuleto's Trattoria*
Kyo-Ya*
La Bergerie*
La Fiammetta
La Folie
La Forêt/S*
La Ginestra*
La Mère Michelle/S*
La Petite Auberge
Lark Creek Inn*
La Scene*
Le Club*
Le Mouton Noir/S*
Le Papillon/S*
Leticia's*
Liberté*
Lion & Compass/S*
Little City*
L'Olivier*
London Wine Bar*
LuLuBis/Cafe/Rest.*
MacArthur Park*
Madrona Manor/N*
Maharani India*
Mama's*
Mamounia*
Mandalay
Mandarin House*
Mandarin, The*
Marin Joe's*
Marrakech*
Masa's*
Maxfield's B & G
Maye's Hse.*
Mayflower
McCormick/Kutelo*
Meadowood Rest./N*
Metropole*
Mifune
Milano Pizzeria
Miss Pearl's Jam*
Mom Is Cooking*
Moose's*
Mozarella di Bufala
Narai
Narsai's Cafe
New Joe's
Nob Hill*
North Beach*
North India*
North Sea Village*
Occidental Grill
Ocean Restaurant*
O Chame
Old Swiss House*
Olive's Pizza
Oliveto*
One Market*
Osome*
Pacific Fresh/S*
Pacific Grill*
Pacific Heights*
Pacific's Edge/S*
Palermo/S*
Palio D'Asti*

Palomino
Paolo's/S*
Park Grill*
Parma
Pasta Moon/S*
Pasta Prego/N
Pauline's Pizza*
Pavilion*
Perry's*
Piazza D'Angelo*
Plearn Thai*
Plumed Horse/S*
Plump Jack Cafe*
Postrio*
Prego
Rasselas*
Rendezvous*
Restaurant Enoteca*
Rice Table
Rio Grill/S
Rist. Ecco
Rist. Lucca*
Rist. Milano
Ritz-Carlton Din. Rm.*
Roti*
Rotunda, The
Rubicon
Rue de Main *
Sally's
Samba Java/N
Sam's Grill*
Samui Thai
Sardine Factory/S*
Savannah Grill*
Schroeder's*
Scoma's*
Scott's Seafood*
Sears Fine Foods
Seoul Garden*
Sherman House*
Showley's/N*
Siam Cuisine
Silks*
Spiedini
Splendido's*
Square One*
Stanford Park*
Stars Cafe*
Stars Oakville/N*
Station House*
Stinking Rose*
Sunset Dining Rm./S
Tadich Grill
Taiwan
Tanuki
Tarantino's
Tarpy's Roadhouse/S*
Terra/N*
Thornhill Cafe*
Ti Bacio
Tommy's Joynt
Tommy Toy's*
Ton Kiang*
Tortola
Tourelle Cafe*
Tratt. Contadina*
Tra Vigne/N*
Tre Scalini/N
231 Ellsworth
U.S. Restaurant*
Umberto*
Vanessi's*
Venezia*
Venticello
Vic Stewart's*
Vince S.F.*
Vivande Porta Via
¡Wa-Ha-Ka!*
Waterfront, The
Wente Bros.*
Woodward's Garden
Wu Kong*
Yamato*
Yank Sing
Yet Wah
Yoshida-Ya*
Yoshi's*
Yuet Lee
Yujean's*
Zax
Zza's Tratt.*

People-Watching

Act IV
Alfred's
A. Sabella's
Avalon

Avenue Grill
Bahia
Bix
Blue Light
Boulevard
Buckeye Roadhse.
Cafe Chez Panisse
Cafe Flore
Cafe Marimba
Caribbean Zone
Chez Panisse
Chez T.J.
Club 181
Cypress Club
Eleven Rist. & Bar
Embarko
Enrico's
Fly Trap
Fog City Diner
Garden Court
Gordon Biersch
Guaymas
Hamburger Mary's
Hard Rock Cafe
Harry Denton's
Hayes St. Grill
Julie's
La Mère Michelle
LuLuBis/Cafe/Rest.
Mandarin, The
Max's Opera Cafe
Moose's
One Market
Park Grill
Perry's
Postrio
Regina's
Rotunda, The
Rubicon
Square One
Stars Cafe
Washington Sq. B & G
Zuni Cafe

Power Scenes

Alain Rondelli
Aqua
Big Four
Bix
Boulevard
Chez Panisse
Cypress Club
Hayes St. Grill
La Folie
Lion & Compass/S
LuLuBis/Cafe/Rest.
Masa's
Moose's
Park Grill
Postrio
Stars
Washington Sq. B & G
Zuni Cafe

Pre-Theater Menus

(Call to check prices, days and times)

Avalon
Beausejour/S
Cafe Adriano
Cafe Mozart
California Cafe/N
Campton Place
Eastside Oyster/N
Emporio Armani
Fly Trap
Fournou's Ovens
Garden Court
Gira Polli
Kiss
La Petite Auberge
La Scene
Le Cyrano
Little Italy
North India
Paolo's/S
Ritz-Carlton Din. Rm.
Sardine Factory/S
Saul's Deli
Scott's Seafood
Ti Bacio
Tourelle Cafe
Vic Stewart's
Victor's

Prix Fixe Menus

(Call to check prices, days and times)

Alain Rondelli
Alexander

Amelio's
Aqua
Baker St. Bistro
Beausejour/S
Bella Voce
Brasserie Savoy
Cafe Chez Panisse
Caffe Sport
Cal. Cul. Academy
California Cafe/N
Campton Place
Capp's Corner
Carnelian Room
Chez Panisse
China Moon Cafe
Emile's/S
Emporio Armani
ERIC Restaurant
Erna's House/S
Esperpento
Eulipia/S
French Laundry/N
French Room
Goro's Robato
Greens
Grille/N
Kansai
La Bergerie
La Folie
Lalime's
La Mère Michelle/S
La Scene
Le Mouton Noir/S
Le Trou
L'Olivier
LuLuBis/Cafe/Rest.
Madrona Manor/N
Mandalay
Mandarin, The
Masa's
Metropole
Napa Vall. Wine/N
Narai
Nob Hill
North India
One Market
Pacific's Edge/S
Paolo's/S
PJ's Oyster Bed
Rist. Fabrizio
Rubicon
Samui Thai
Sardine Factory/S
Scott's Seafood
Sherman House
Sierra Mar/S
Silks
South Park Cafe
Splendido's
Straits Cafe
Taiwan
Ton Kiang
Tourelle Cafe
Trilogy/N
231 Ellsworth
U.S. Restaurant
Wente Bros.
Yamato
Yank Sing
Yujean's

Pubs/Bars

Gordon Biersch
Los Gatos/S
Pacific T & G
Tommy's Joynt

Quiet Conversation

Alioto's
Amelio's
Bella Vista
Eastside Oyster/N
El Paseo
Fournou's Ovens
Garden Court
John Ash & Co./N
Madrona Manor/N
Masa's
Napa Vall. Wine/N
Ritz-Carlton Din. Rm.
San Benito Hse./S
Sherman House
Silks
Trilogy/N
231 Ellsworth

Reservations Essential

Act IV
Adriatic

Alain Rondelli
Alexander
Alta Mira
Amelio's
Angkor Wat
Anjou
Aux Delices
Avenue Grill
Bacco
Balboa Cafe
Beausejour/S
Bella Vista
Benihana
Bistro D. Giovanni/N
Boulevard
Bridges
Buca Giovanni
Buffalo Grill
Cafe Chez Panisse
Cafe Beaujolais/N
Cafe de Bordeaux
Cafe Jacqueline
Cafe Maisonnette
Cafe Mozart
Cafe 222
Caffe Roma
Caffe Sport
Cal. Cul. Academy
Campton Place
Caribbean Zone
Carnelian Room
Carrara's Cafe
Casanova/S
Castagnola's
Catahoula/N
Chambord
Chateau Souverain/N
Cheer's Cafe
Chef Chu's/S
Chevys
Chez Panisse
Chez T.J.
China Moon Cafe
Ciao Ristorante
City of Paris
Club XIX/S
Courtyard B & G
Crustacean
Dal Baffo
Delancey St.
Doidge's
Domaine Chandon/N
Dusit Thai
El Tapatio
Embarko
Emerald Garden
Emile's/S
Emporio Armani
Empress of China
Enrico's
Erna's House/S
Ernesto's
Esperpento
Eulipia/S
Fana Ethiopian
Firefly
Fleur de Lys
Flower Lounge
Flying Saucer
Fly Trap
Foothill Cafe/N
Fountain Court
French Laundry/N
French Room
Fresh Cream/S
Fringale
Fung Lum/S
Garden Court
Gertie's
Gervais/S
Geva's
Ginger Island
Goro's Robato
Guaymas
Gulf Coast G & B
Harris'
Hayes St. Grill
Helmand
Hunan Rest.
Hyde St. Bistro
Iberia
Il Fornaio
Imperial Palace
Iron Horse
Izzy's Steak
Jackson Fillmore
Jin Jiang Kee Joon
Johnny Love's

Julius' Castle
Kabuto Sushi
Kansai
Kelly's on Trinity
King Charcoal BBQ
King of China
Korea House
Kyo-Ya
La Bergerie
La Folie
La Pergola
La Scene
Le Central Bistro
Le Club
Le Mouton Noir/S
L'Entrecote
Leticia's
Le Trou
Liberté
Lichee Garden
Little Henry's
Little Italy
Little Joe's
London Wine Bar
Los Gatos/S
MacArthur Park
Madrona Manor/N
Mamounia
Mandalay
Mandarin House
Manora's Thai
Marin Joe's
Masa's
Maxfield's B & G
Maye's Hse.
Mayflower
Meadowood Rest./N
Mo's Burgers
Mom Is Cooking
Moose's
Mustards Grill/N
Napa Vall. Wine/N
Narai
New Joe's
North Beach
North Sea Village
Ocean Restaurant
O Chame
Old Swiss House
Orig. Old Clam Hse.
Osome
Osteria
Pacific Fresh/S
Pacific Heights
Pacific's Edge/S
Palermo/S
Palomino
Parma
Pasta Moon/S
Pasta Prego/N
Pavilion
Perry's
Piatti/N
Piazza D'Angelo
Pier 23 Cafe
Plearn Thai
Plumed Horse/S
Plump Jack Cafe
Postrio
Prego
Rasselas
Restaurant Enoteca
Rio Grill/S
Rist. Lucca
Rist. Ecco
Rist. Milano
Ritz-Carlton Din. Rm.
Ritz-Carlton Terr.
Roosevelt Tamale
Royal Thai
Rubicon
Rue de Main
Samba Java/N
San Benito Hse./S
San Francisco BBQ
Sand Dollar
Santa Fe B & G
Schroeder's
Sears Fine Foods
Sherman House
Sierra Mar/S
Sol y Luna
South Park Cafe
Stanford Park
Suppenkuche
Taiwan
Tarantino's
Tarpy's Roadhouse/S

Tommy Toy's
Tortola
Tratt. Contadina
Tre Scalini/N
Trilogy/N
Tu Lan
231 Ellsworth
U.S. Restaurant
Umberto
Venticello
Victor's
Woodward's Garden
Wu Kong
Yet Wah
Yoshida-Ya
Yoshi's
Yuet Lee

Reservations Not Accepted
(Check for larger parties)
Ace Cafe
Asimakopoulos
Bette's Oceanview
Bucci's
Cafe Flore
Cafe/All Seasons
Cal. Pizza Kit.
Cha Cha Cha's
Ciao Ristorante
Cordon Bleu
Dottie's Cafe
Ebisu
Edokko
Elite Cafe, The
Eric's Chinese
Fana Ethiopian
Fat Apple's
Gray Whale
Guernica
Hahn's Hibachi
Hard Rock Cafe
Horizons
House of Nanking
Indian Oven
Iroha
Isobune Sushi
JoAnn's Cafe
Kirala
Kiss
La Cumbre
La Mediterranee
La Taqueria
LuLuBis/Cafe/Rest.
Mario's Bohemian
Max's Opera Cafe
Mel's Drive-In
Mifune
Narsai's Cafe
North India
Olive's Pizza
Osome
Pacific Cafe
Paragon
Pauline's Pizza
Rasselas
Rendezvous
Rio Grill/S
Sally's
Samba Java/N
Sam's Grill
Sanppo
Saul's Deli
Scoma's
South China Cafe
Spuntino
Swan Oyster Depot
Tadich Grill
Tanuki
Taqueria Mission
Ti Couz
Tommaso's
Tommy's Joynt
Trio Cafe
Vivande Porta Via
¡Wa-Ha-Ka!
Zachary's

Romantic Spots
Acquerello
Act IV
Alain Rondelli
Amelio's
Barbarossa
Bella Vista
Buca Giovanni
Cafe Jacqueline
Cafe Maisonnette

Cafe Majestic
Cafe Mozart
Campbell House/S
Casa Madrona
Casanova/S
Covey, The/S
Domaine Chandon/N
Eastside Oyster/N
El Paseo
Erna's House/S
Fleur de Lys
French Room
Fresh Cream/S
John Ash & Co./N
La Folie
La Petite Auberge
Lark Creek Inn
L'Olivier
Madrona Manor/N
Maharani India
Masa's
Meadowood Rest./N
Pacific's Edge/S
San Benito Hse./S
Showley's/N
Sierra Mar/S
Terra/N
French Laundry/N
Ti Bacio
Tre Scalini/N
Trilogy/N
231 Ellsworth
Woodward's Garden

Saturday – Best Bets
(B = brunch; L = lunch; best of many)
Abiquiu (L)
Acorn Tea (B)
A La Carte (L)
Alexander (L)
Alioto's (L)
Anjou (L)
A. Sabella's (L)
Auberge du Soleil/N (L)
Avalon (L)
Baker St. Bistro (B,L)
Barnaby's By Bay (L)
Basta Pasta (L)
Bella Voce (L)
Bette's Oceanview (L)
Bill's Place (L)
Bistro D. Giovanni/N (L)
Blue Chalk Cafe (L)
Bocce Cafe (B,L)
Brother's Deli (L)
Buchanan Grill (B)
Buckeye Roadhse. (L)
Cactus Cafe (L)
Cadillac Bar (L)
Cafe Akimbo (L)
Cafe Bastille (L)
Cafe Claude (L)
Cafe de Bordeaux (L)
Cafe Fanny (L)
Cafe/All Seasons (B)
Cafe Majestic (B,L)
Cafe Marimba (B,L)
Cafe Mozart (L)
Cafe 222 (B,L)
Caffe Delle Stelle (L)
California Cafe/N (L)
Campton Place (L)
Capp's Corner (L)
Caprice, The (L)
Caribbean Zone (L)
Carnelian Room (B,L)
Casa Aguila (L)
Casanova/S (L)
Catahoula/N (B,L)
Central 159/S (L)
Ciao Ristorante (L)
Clark's By Bay (L)
Clement St. B & G (B,L)
Cliff House (L)
Crow's Nest/S (L)
Curbside Cafe (B,L)
Delancey St. (L)
Doidge's (B,L)
Domaine Chandon/N (L)
Doug's BBQ (L)
Eastside Oyster/N (L)
Ebisu (L)
Edokko (L)
Elka (L)
Emporio Armani (L)
Eulipia/S (L)
Fior D'Italia (L)

Fly Trap (L)
Fog City Diner (L)
Fournou's Ovens (B)
French Laundry/N (L)
Garden Court (B)
Gate Five (B,L)
Ginger Island (B)
Golden Turtle (L)
Gordon Biersch (L)
Goro's Robato (L)
Gray Whale (L)
Greens (L)
Grille/N (L)
Guaymas (L)
Gulf Coast G & B (B)
Hamburger Mary's (B,L)
Harbor Village (L)
Harry Denton's (B,L)
Helmand (L)
Horizons (B,L)
House of Nanking (L)
Iron Horse (L)
Island Cafe (B,L)
Jade Villa (B,L)
JoAnn's B Street (B,L)
JoAnn's Cafe (B,L)
John Ash & Co./N (L)
Kansai (L)
Kelly's on Trinity (L)
Kenwood/N (L)
Kim's (L)
Kirala (L)
Kirin (L)
Kiss (L)
Kuleto's Italian (L)
Kyo-Ya (L)
La Mediterranee (L)
La Mère Michelle/S (B,L)
La Petite Auberge (L)
Le Central Bistro (L)
Le Mouton Noir/S (L)
Liberté (L)
Little City (L)
London Wine Bar (L)
Long Life Vegi Hse. (B,L)
Los Gatos/S (B)
LuLuBis/Cafe/Rest. (L)
MacArthur Park (L)
Maharani India (L)
Mama's (L)
Mama's Royal Cafe (B)
Mandarin House (L)
Mandarin, The (L)
Manora's Thai (L)
Marin Joe's (L)
Mario's Bohemian (L)
Marnee Thai (L)
Maxfield's B & G (L)
Max's Diner (L)
McCormick/Kuleto (L)
Meadowood Rest./N (L)
Mel's Drive-In (L)
Mustards Grill/N (L)
Nan Yang (L)
Napa Vall. Wine/N (L)
Nob Hill (L)
Orig. Old Clam Hse. (B)
Original Joe's (L)
Pacific Fresh/S (L)
Pacific T & G (L)
Pacific's Edge/S (B)
Palermo/S (L)
Palomino (B,L)
Pane e Vino (L)
Park Grill (B,L)
Pasta Moon/S (L)
Pasta Prego/N (L)
Pauli's Cafe (B)
Pavilion (B)
Phnom Penh (L)
Piatti/N (L)
Pier 23 Cafe (L)
PJ's Oyster Bed (L)
Postrio (B)
Prego (L)
Primo Patio Cafe (B,L)
Rio Grill/S (L)
Rist. Fabrizio (L)
Roosevelt Tamale (L)
Rosmarino (L)
Rotunda, The (L)
Royal Thai (L)
Rue de Main (L)
Sally's (B,L)
Samba Java/N (L)
Sam's Anchor (B,L)
Samui Thai (L)

San Benito Hse./S (B)
Sand Dollar (B)
San Francisco BBQ (L)
Sanppo (L)
Saul's Deli (L)
Savannah Grill (L)
Schroeder's (L)
Scott's Seafood (B,L)
Sherman House (L)
Showley's/N (L)
Siam Cuisine (L)
Sierra Mar/S (L)
Silks (B)
Sol y Luna (L)
Splendido's (L)
Spuntino (B,L)
Stars Cafe (B)
Stars Oakville/N (L)
Station House (L)
Stinking Rose (L)
Straits Cafe (L)
Sunset Dining Rm./S (L)
Swan Oyster Depot (B,L)
Tanuki (L)
Tarpy's Roadhouse/S (B,L)
Thornhill Cafe (B,L)
Ti Couz (B)
Tommy's Joynt (L)
Tommy Toy's (L)
Vicolo Pizzeria (L)
Vince S.F. (B)
¡Wa-Ha-Ka! (B,L)
Washington Sq. B & G (L)
Waterfront, The (L)
Wente Bros. (L)
Yoshida-Ya (L)
Yujean's (L)
Zachary's (L)
Zuni Cafe (L)

Sunday – Best Bets

(B = Brunch; L = Lunch; D = Dinner; plus all hotels and most Asians)

Abiquiu (L,D)
Ace Cafe (D)
Acorn Tea (B)
Adriana's/N (D)
A La Carte (L,D)
Alain Rondelli (D)
Alejandro's (D)
Alexander (L,D)
Alfred's (D)
Allegro (D)
Alta Mira (B,D)
Amelio's (D)
Angkor Wat (L)
Appam (D)
A. Sabella's (L,D)
Asimakopoulos (D)
Avalon (D)
Baci Caffe (D)
Bahia (D)
Baker St. Bistro (B,L)
Barnaby's By Bay (B,D)
Basta Pasta (L,D)
Bay Wolf (D)
Bette's Oceanview (B,L)
Bill's Place (B,L,D)
Bistro Clovis (L)
Bistro D. Giovanni/N (L,D)
Bix (D)
Blue Chalk Cafe (L,D)
Blue Light (B,D)
Bocce Cafe (B,L,D)
Bonta (D)
Boulevard (D)
Bridges (D)
Brother's Deli (B,L,D)
Buca Giovanni (D)
Buchanan Grill (B,D)
Buckeye Roadhse. (B,L,D)
Buffalo Grill (I)
Cacti Grill (D)
Cactus Cafe (L,D)
Cadillac Bar (L,D)
Cafe Adriano (D)
Cafe Chez Panisse (L,D)
Cafe de Bordeaux (L,D)
Cafe Fanny (B,L)
Cafe/All Seasons (B,D)
Cafe Kati (D)
Cafe Maisonnette (D)
Cafe Marimba (B,L,D)
Cafe Mozart (B,L,D)
Cafe Riggio (D)
Caffe Sport (L,D)
California Cafe/N (B,D)

Campbell House/S (D)
Capellini (D)
Capp's Corner (L,D)
Caprice, The (B,D)
Caribbean Zone (L,D)
Carrara's Cafe (B,L,D)
Casa Aguila (B,L,D)
Casa Madrona
Casanova/S (B,D)
Chambord (L,D)
Chez Panisse (L,D)
China House (D)
Ciao Ristorante (D)
Citron (D)
Clark's By Bay (L,D)
Clement St. B & G (B,D)
Cliff House (B,L,D)
Club 181 (D)
Courtyard B & G (B)
Curbside Cafe (B,L,D)
Cypress Club (D)
Delancey St. (L,D)
Doidge's (B,L)
Domaine Chandon/N (L,D)
Doug's BBQ (L,D)
Downtown Bakery/N (B)
Eastside Oyster/N (B,L,D)
Ebisu (L,D)
Edokko (L)
Elite Cafe, The (B,D)
El Paseo (D)
Embarko (D)
Emerald Garden (D)
Enrico's (D)
Erna's House/S (B,D)
Eulipia/S (L)
Fana Ethiopian (D)
Fior D'Italia (L,D)
Flea St. Cafe (B,D)
Fly Trap (L,D)
Fog City Diner (L,D)
French Laundry/N (L,D)
Fresh Cream/S (D)
Garibaldi (B,D)
Gate Five (B,L,D)
Gertie's (D)
Geva's (D)
Ginger Island (L)
Gira Polli (D)
Golden Turtle (L,D)
Gordon Biersch (L,D)
Goro's Robato (L)
Gray Whale (L,D)
Greens (B)
Guaymas (B,D)
Guernica (D)
Hamburger Mary's (B,L,D)
Harris' (D)
Hayes St. Grill (D)
Helmand (L)
Horizons (B,L,D)
House of Nanking (L,D)
House of Prime Rib (D)
I Fratelli (D)
Iron Horse (D)
Ivy's (B,D)
Jade Villa (B,L,D)
JoAnn's B Street (B,L)
JoAnn's Cafe (B,L)
John Ash & Co./N (B,L,D)
Kansai (L,D)
Kenwood/N (L,D)
Khan Toke Thai (D)
Kim's (L)
Kirala (L)
Kirin (L,D)
Kuleto's Trattoria (L,D)
La Fiammetta (D)
La Forêt/S (B,D)
Laghi (D)
La Ginestra (D)
Lalime's (D)
La Mère Michelle/S (B,L,D)
La Petite Auberge (B,L,D)
Lark Creek Inn (B,D)
La Scene (B)
Le Club (D)
Le Cyrano (D)
Le Mouton Noir/S (D)
Le Papillon/S (D)
Leticia's (B)
Le Trou (D)
Liberté (L)
Little City (L,D)
London Wine Bar (L,D)
Long Life Vegi Hse. (B,L,D)
Los Gatos/S (L)
LuLuBis/Cafe/Rest. (D)

MacArthur Park (L)
Maharani India (L,D)
Mama's Royal Cafe (B)
Mandarin House (L,D)
Manora's Thai (L)
Marin Joe's (L)
Mario's Bohemian (B,L,D)
Marnee Thai (L,D)
Marrakech (D)
Max's Diner (L,D)
Mel's Drive-In (B,L,D)
Mescolanza (D)
Metropole (D)
Miss Pearl's Jam (B,D)
Mustards Grill/N (L,D)
Nan Yang (L,D)
Napa Vall. Wine/N (B,L,D)
North India (D)
O Chame (L,D)
Oliveto (D)
Omnivore (D)
One Market (B,D)
Original Joe's (B,L,D)
Oritalia (D)
Osome (D)
Osteria (D)
Pacific Cafe (D)
Pacific Fresh/S (L)
Pacific T & G (B,L,D)
Palermo/S (L)
Pane e Vino (D)
Paragon (D)
Parma (D)
Pasta Moon/S (L,D)
Pauli's Cafe (B,D)
Phnom Penh (D)
Piatti/N (L,D)
Pier 23 Cafe (B)
PJ's Oyster Bed (B,L,D)
Prego (L,D)
Primo Patio Cafe (B,L)
Rasselas (D)
Regina's (D)
Restaurant Enoteca (D)
Rice Table (D)
Rio Grill/S (B,L,D)
Rist. Fabrizio (B,L,D)
Rist. Lucca (D)
Rist. Milano (D)
Rivoli Restaurant (D)
Roosevelt Tamale (L,D)
Rosmarino (B)
Royal Thai (L)
Ruby's (D)
Rue de Main (L,D)
Sally's (B)
Samba Java/N (B,L)
Sam's Anchor (B,L,D)
Samui Thai (D)
San Francisco BBQ (L)
Sanppo (D)
Santa Fe B & G (D)
Sardine Factory/S (D)
Saul's Deli (B,L,D)
Savannah Grill (L,D)
Schroeder's (L,D)
Scott's Seafood (B,L,D)
Showley's/N (L,D)
Siam Cuisine (D)
Sol y Luna (L,D)
South China Cafe (L)
Spiedini (D)
Spuntino (B,L,D)
Square One (D)
Stars (D)
Stars Cafe (B,D)
Stars Oakville/N (L,D)
Station House (B,L,D)
Stinking Rose (L,D)
Straits Cafe (B,L,D)
Suppenkuche (L)
Tadich Grill (L,D)
Tanuki (L)
Tarpy's Roadhouse/S (L)
Terra/N (D)
Thornhill Cafe (B,L,D)
Ti Bacio (D)
Ti Couz (B,D)
Tommaso's (D)
Tommy Toy's (L)
Tommy's Joynt (L,D)
Tortola (L)
Tourelle Cafe (B,D)
Tratt. Contadina (D)
Tra Vigne/N (B)
Tre Fratelli (D)

Tre Scalini/N (D)
Trilogy/N (D)
Tu Lan (L,D)
U.S. Restaurant (B,L,D)
Vanessi's (D)
Venezia (D)
Venticello (D)
Vicolo Pizzeria (L,D)
Vic Stewart's (D)
Vince S.F. (B,D)
¡Wa-Ha-Ka! (L,D)
Washington Sq. B & G (D)
Waterfront, The (B,L,D)
Wente Bros. (B,L,D)
Woodward's Garden (D)
Yamato (D)
Yoshida-Ya (L)
Yujean's (L,D)
Zachary's (L,D)
Zuni Cafe (B,L,D)
Zza's Tratt. (D)

Senior Appeal

Alfred's
Alioto's
Bardelli's
Garden Court
Harris'
House of Prime Rib
La Petite Auberge
La Mère Michelle/S
Marin Joe's
Scoma's
Sears Fine Foods

Singles Scenes

Abiquiu
Ace Cafe
Aqua
Avalon
Bahia
Balboa Cafe
Bix
Blue Light
Buchanan Grill
Cadillac Bar
Cafe Flore
Caribbean Zone
Cava 555
Chevys
Ciao Ristorante
Clark's By Bay
Clement St. B & G
Club 181
Crow's Nest/S
Cypress Club
Eleven Rist. & Bar
Elite Cafe, The
Embarko
Fog City Diner
Garibaldi
Gordon Biersch
Guaymas
Hamburger Mary's
Harry Denton's
Hunan Rest.
Il Fornaio
Ivy's
Johnny Love's
Julie's
Kuleto's Italian
Leticia's
Liberté
London Wine Bar
LuLuBis/Cafe/Rest.
MacArthur Park
Metropole
Miss Pearl's Jam
Moose's
Pacific Heights
Palomino
Paragon
Perry's
Postrio
Prego
Rasselas
Regina's
Sam's Anchor
Sol y Luna
Stars
Stars Cafe
Umberto
Vanessi's
Washington Sq. B & G
Zuni Cafe

Sleepers
(Good to excellent food, but little known)

Alexander
Baker St. Bistro
Barbarossa
Beausejour/S
Cacti Grill
Cactus Cafe
Cafe Akimbo
Cafe Maisonnette
Campbell House/S
Central 159/S
Chez Renee/S
Club XIX/S
Covey, The/S
Cypress Club
Dottie's Cafe
Downtown Bakery/N
Dusit Thai
Eleven Rist. & Bar
Emile's/S
Eric's Chinese
Erna's House/S
Foothill Cafe/N
Gervais/S
Geva's
Goro's Robato
Grille/N
Guernica
Hahn's Hibachi
Half Shell
Imperial Palace
Indian Oven
JoAnn's Cafe
King Charcoal BBQ
Kirala
Korea House
Kyo-Ya
La Bergerie
La Forêt/S
La Mère Michelle/S
La Petite Auberge
La Traviata
Le Cyrano
Le Marquis
Le Papillon/S
Liberté
Lichee Garden
Lion & Compass/S
Los Gatos/S
Madrona Manor/N
Mamounia
Marrakech
Maxfield's B & G
Mo's Burgers
Nadine's
Nan Yang
Narai
Nob Hill
North Sea Village
Occidental Grill
Ocean Restaurant
Omnivore
Osome
Paolo's/S
Pasta Prego/N
Phnom Penh
Plumed Horse/S
Primo Patio Cafe
Regina's
Rendezvous
Rice Table
Rist. Fabrizio
Rue de Main
Samui Thai
San Benito Hse./S
Sanppo
Showley's/N
Siam Cuisine
Sierra Mar/S
Station House
Suppenkuche
Tanuki
Taqueria Mission
Tarpy's Roadhouse/S
Thornhill Cafe
Tre Scalini/N
Trilogy/N
Trio Cafe
Tu Lan
Vic Stewart's
Victor's
Yoshida-Ya
Yuet Lee
Zax

Teflons

(Gets lots of business, despite so-so food, i.e. they have other attractions that prevent criticism from sticking)

Cadillac Bar
Cliff House
Julius' Castle
Mel's Drive-In
Spenger's Fish

Smoking Prohibited

(May be permissible at bar or outdoors)

Acorn Tea
Acquerello
Adriana's/N
Alain Rondelli
Allegro
Amelio's
Anjou
Appam
Asimakopoulos
Avenue Grill
Bacco
Baci Caffe
Baker St. Bistro
Barnaby's By Bay
Bay Wolf
Bette's Oceanview
Bistro D. Giovanni/N
Blue Chalk Cafe
Bonta
Boulevard
Brava Terrace/N
Bridges
Brother's Deli
Buca Giovanni
Buffalo Grill
Cactus Cafe
Cafe Adriano
Cafe Akimbo
Cafe Chez Panisse
Cafe Beaujolais/N
Cafe de Bordeaux
Cafe Fanny
Cafe Jacqueline
Cafe Kati
Cafe Maisonnette
Caffe Delle Stelle
Caffe Macaroni
Cal. Cul. Academy
Cal. Pizza Kit.
California Cafe/N
Campbell House/S
Campton Place
Capellini
Caprice, The
Casa Aguila
Casa Madrona
Castagnola's
Catahoula/N
Central 159/S
Cha Cha Cha's
Chateau Souverain/N
Cheer's Cafe
Chez Panisse
Chez Renee/S
Chez T.J.
China House
China Moon Cafe
Citron
Club XIX/S
Cordon Bleu
Crow's Nest/S
Curbside Cafe
Dal Baffo
Delancey St.
Doidge's
Ebisu
Edokko
El Tapatio
Elka
Emile's/S
Emerald Garden
ERIC Restaurant
Erna's House/S
Ernesto's
Eulipia/S
Fana Ethiopian
Fat Apple's
Fior D'Italia
Firefly
Flower Lounge
Foothill Cafe/N
French Laundry/N
Fresh Cream/S
Fringale

Fung Lum/S
Gertie's
Gervais/S
Geva's
Ginger Island
Gira Polli
Goro's Robato
Gray Whale
Greens
Grille/N
Grissini
Gulf Coast G & B
Hahn's Hibachi
Harris'
Helmand
Hyde St. Bistro
I Fratelli
Iroha
Island Cafe
Isobune Sushi
Ivy's
Jack's
Jackson Fillmore
JoAnn's Cafe
John Ash & Co./N
Julius' Castle
Khan Toke Thai
Kim's
King Charcoal BBQ
Kirala
Kirin
Kiss
La Bergerie
La Fiammetta
La Forêt/S
Laghi
La Ginestra
Lalime's
La Mediterranee
La Pergola
La Scene
La Taqueria
La Traviata
Le Club
Le Cyrano
Le Marquis
Le Mouton Noir/S
Le Trou
Liberté
Little City
Little Italy
Little Joe's
Long Life Vegi Hse.
Los Gatos/S
Mama's Royal Cafe
Mamounia
Mandalay
Mandarin House
Masa's
Maxfield's B & G
McCormick/Kutelo
Meadowood Rest./N
Mescolanza
Metropole
Mifune
Mustards Grill/N
Nadine's
Nan Yang
Narsai's Cafe
North Sea Village
O Chame
Olive's Pizza
Oliveto
Omnivore
Oritalia
Osteria
Pacific Cafe
Palomino
Pane e Vino
Parma
Pasta Moon/S
Pasta Prego/N
Pauli's Cafe
Pavilion
Phnom Penh
Piatti/N
Piazza D'Angelo
PJ's Oyster Bed
Plearn Thai
Plumed Horse/S
Rendezvous
Restaurant Enoteca
Rice Table
Rist. Fabrizio
Rist. Lucca
Ritz-Carlton Terr.
Rivoli Restaurant
Roosevelt Tamale

Rosmarino
Royal Thai
Ruby's
Sally's
Samba Java/N
Sam's Anchor
San Benito Hse./S
Sand Dollar
San Francisco BBQ
Sanppo
Santa Fe B & G
Saul's Deli
Savannah Grill
Showley's/N
Siam Cuisine
Sierra Mar/S
Sol y Luna
Spiedini
Square One
Straits Cafe
Taiwan
Terra/N
Thep Phanom
Thornhill Cafe
Ti Bacio
Ti Couz
Tortola
Tra Vigne/N
Tre Scalini/N
Trilogy/N
Trio Cafe
231 Ellsworth
Vanessi's
Venezia
Venticello
Vicolo Pizzeria
Victor's
Vivande Porta Via
Woodward's Garden
Yoshi's
Yujean's
Zachary's
Zax
Zza's Tratt.

Teas

Acorn Tea
Act IV
Fournou's Ovens
French Room
Garden Court
Meadowood Rest./N
Nob Hill
Park Grill
Rotunda, The
Sherman House
Station House

Teenagers & Other Youthful Spirits

Benihana
Bill's Place
Cacti Grill
Cactus Cafe
Cal. Pizza Kit.
Campo Santo
Caribbean Zone
Enrico's
Fat Apple's
Fog City Diner
Gira Polli
Gray Whale
Hamburger Mary's
Hard Rock Cafe
JoAnn's B Street
Kabuto Sushi
La Mediterranee
La Taqueria
Mario's Bohemian
Max's Diner
Mel's Drive-In
Miss Pearl's Jam
Mo's Burgers
Pier 23 Cafe
Primo Patio Cafe
U.S. Restaurant

Visitors on Expense Accounts

Acquerello
Alain Rondelli
Amelio's
Big Four
Ernie's
Fleur de Lys
Fournou's Ovens
Garden Court
Harris'

John Ash & Co./N
Julius' Castle
La Folie
Lark Creek Inn
Le Club
Mandarin, The
McCormick/Kutelo
One Market
Pacific's Edge/S
Park Grill
Ritz-Carlton Din. Rm.
Rubicon
Sherman House
Silks
Square One
Victor's

Waterside

Alta Mira
Barnaby's By Bay
Caprice, The
Casa Madrona
Castagnola's
Cliff House
Club XIX/S
Covey, The/S
Crow's Nest/S
Embarko
Fresh Cream/S
Gate Five
Gaylord/Ghirardelli
Gray Whale
Greens
Guaymas
Harry Denton's
Horizons
La Forêt/S
Lark Creek Inn
Mandarin, The
North Sea Village
Old Swiss House
Pier 23 Cafe
Sam's Anchor
Scoma's
Sierra Mar/S
Splendido's
Sunset Dining Rm./S
Tarantino's
Waterfront, The
Yet Wah

Wine/Beer Only

Acorn Tea
Acquerello
Adriana's/N
Adriatic
A La Carte
Allegro
Appam
Asimakopoulos
Aux Delices
Bacco
Baci Caffe
Bahia
Baker St. Bistro
Barnaby's By Bay
Bay Wolf
Bill's Place
Bistro Clovis
Bonta
Brother's Deli
Buca Giovanni
Bucci's
Cactus Cafe
Cafe Adriano
Cafe Akimbo
Cafe Chez Panisse
Cafe Beaujolais/N
Cafe Claude
Cafe de Bordeaux
Cafe Fanny
Cafe Flore
Cafe/All Seasons
Cafe Jacqueline
Cafe Kati
Cafe Maisonnette
Cafe Mozart
Caffe Delle Stelle
Caffe Greco
Caffe Macaroni
Caffe Sport
Cal. Roastery
Campbell House/S
Campo Santo
Carrara's Cafe
Casa Aguila
Casa Madrona
Casanova/S
Central 159/S

Cha Cha Cha's
Chateau Souverain/N
Cheer's Cafe
Chez Panisse
Chez T.J.
China Moon Cafe
Citron
Curbside Cafe
Delancey St.
Doidge's
Domaine Chandon/N
Dottie's Cafe
Dusit Thai
Eastside Oyster/N
Ebisu
Edokko
El Paseo
Emerald Garden
Eric's Chinese
Ernesto's
Esperpento
Fana Ethiopian
Fat Apple's
Firefly
Flea St. Cafe
Flower Lounge
Flying Saucer
Foothill Cafe/N
Fountain Court
French Laundry/N
Gertie's
Geva's
Gira Polli
Golden Turtle
Gordon Biersch
Goro's Robato
Gray Whale
Greens
Guernica
Gulf Coast G & B
Hahn's Hibachi
House of Nanking
Hyde St. Bistro
I Fratelli
Indian Oven
Iroha
Island Cafe
Isobune Sushi
Jackson Fillmore
Jade Villa
JoAnn's Cafe
Kabuto Sushi
Kelly's on Trinity
Kim's
King Charcoal BBQ
Kirala
Kirin
Kiss
Korea House
La Bergerie
La Cumbre
La Fiammetta
Laghi
Lalime's
La Mediterranee
La Pergola
La Traviata
Le Trou
Lichee Garden
Little Henry's
Little Italy
Little Joe's
London Wine Bar
Long Life Vegi Hse.
Los Gatos/S
Madrona Manor/N
Mel's Drive-In
Mamounia
Mandalay
Mandarin House
Mario's Bohemian
Marnee Thai
Mel's Drive-In
Mescolanza
Mifune
Milano Pizzeria
Mozarella di Bufala
Nan Yang
Narai
Narsai's Cafe
North Sea Village
Ocean Restaurant
O Chame
Olive's Pizza
Oliveto
Omnivore
Osome
Osteria

Pacific Cafe
Pacific T & G
Panama Hotel
Pane e Vino
Parma
Pasta Moon/S
Pasta Prego/N
Pauline's Pizza
Pauli's Cafe
PJ's Oyster Bed
Plearn Thai
Plump Jack Cafe
Primo Patio Cafe
Rendezvous
Restaurant Enoteca
Rice Table
Rist. Fabrizio
Rist. Lucca
Rist. Milano
Rivoli Restaurant
Roosevelt Tamale
Royal Thai
Ruby's
Rue de Main
Sally's
Samba Java/N
Samui Thai
San Francisco BBQ
Sanppo
Saul's Deli
Sherman House
Showley's/N
Siam Cuisine
South China Cafe
Stars Oakville/N
Suppenkuche
Swan Oyster Depot
Taiwan
Tanuki
Taqueria Mission
Terra/N
Thep Phanom
Thornhill Cafe
Ti Couz
Ton Kiang
Tortola
Tratt. Contadina
Tre Fratelli
Tre Scalini/N
Trilogy/N
Trio Cafe
Tu Lan
231 Ellsworth
U.S. Restaurant
Venezia
Vicolo Pizzeria
Vivande Porta Via
Wente Bros.
Woodward's Garden
Yuet Lee
Yujean's
Zachary's
Zza's Tratt.

Winning Wine Lists

Acquerello
Aqua
Avalon
Auberge du Soleil/N
Balboa Cafe
Bay Wolf
Brava Terrace/N
Cava 555
Chez Panisse
Chez T.J.
Dal Baffo
Domaine Chandon/N
El Paseo
ERIC Restaurant
Ernie's
Flea St. Cafe
Fleur de Lys
Fournou's Ovens
French Laundry/N
French Room
Greens
John Ash & Co./N
Lark Creek Inn
London Wine Bar
Masa's
Meadowood Rest./N
Mustards Grill/N
One Market
Pacific's Edge/S
Postrio
Rist. Ecco
Rubicon

Sardine Factory/S
Silks
Stars
Terra/N
Tra Vigne/N
231 Ellsworth
Victor's
Zuni Cafe

Worth a Trip

NORTH

Marin

Station House

Napa

Auberge du Soleil
Brava Terrace
Domain Chandon
French Laundry
Mustards Grill
Napa Vall. Wine Train
Meadowood Rest.
Terra
Trilogy

Sonoma

Eastside Oyster Bar & Grill
Tre Scalini

SOUTH

Half Moon Bay

San Benito Hse.
Sierra Mar

Monterey/Carmel

Pacific's Edge

Santa Cruz

Chez Renee

San Jose

Emile's
La Mère Michelle

Young Children

(Besides, the normal fast-food places; * indicates children's menu available)

Alexander*
A. Sabella's*
Avalon*
Barnaby's By Bay*
Benihana*
Bill's Place*
Brother's Deli*
Cactus Cafe*
Cafe de Bordeaux*
Caffe Sport*
Cal. Pizza Kit.*
Capellini*
Capp's Corner*
Castagnola's*
Cheer's Cafe
Chevys*
Chez Panisse*
Clark's By Bay*
Crow's Nest/S*
Eastside Oyster/N*
El Tapatio*
Elka*
Esperpento*
Fat Apple's
Fournou's Ovens*
French Room*
Garden Court*
Goro's Robato*
Hamburger Mary's*
Hard Rock Cafe*
Horizons*
House of Prime Rib*
Iberia*
Iroha*
Isobune Sushi*
JoAnn's Cafe*
Kenwood/N*
Kuleto's Trattoria*
La Ginestra*
Lark Creek Inn*
Little Henry's*
Little Joe's*
Los Gatos/S*
Mama's*
Marin Joe's*
Maxfield's B & G*
Max's Diner*
Max's Opera Cafe*
Mel's Drive-In*
New Joe's*
North India*
One Market*
Pacific Fresh/S*
Pacific Grill*
Pacific's Edge/S*
Palomino*
Park Grill*

ALPHABETICAL PAGE INDEX

Wine Vintage Chart 1982-1993

These ratings are designed to help you select wine to go with your meal. They are on the same 0–to–30 scale used throughout this *Survey*. The ratings reflect both the quality of the vintage and the wine's readiness to drink. Thus if a wine is not fully mature or is over the hill, its rating has been reduced. The ratings were prepared principally by our friend Howard Stravitz, a law professor at the University of South Carolina.

WHITES	'82	'83	'85	'86	'87	'88	'89	'90	'91	'92	'93
French:											
Burgundy	23	15	28	29	13	23	29	25	17	26	20
Loire Valley	—	—	18	17	13	18	25	24	17	15	18
Champagne	27	23	28	24	—	—	26	25	—	—	—
Sauternes	—	28	21	26	—	27	26	23	—	—	—
California:											
Chardonnay	—	—	—	—	—	26	19	27	25	28	27
REDS											
French:											
Bordeaux	29	26	28	26	16	25	27	25	18	20	23
Burgundy	19	20	28	12	21	25	26	28	21	24	22
Rhône	15	25	26	21	14	27	27	25	18	16	19
Beaujolais	—	—	—	—	—	20	25	22	24	18	23
California:											
Cabernet/ Merlot	23	14	27	25	25	15	20	25	24	23	23
Zinfandel	—	—	18	17	20	15	16	19	19	18	18
Italian:											
Chianti	16	13	27	15	—	24	—	25	—	—	—
Piedmont	25	—	26	11	18	21	26	26	—	—	19

Bargain sippers take note: Some wines are reliable year in, year out, and are reasonably priced as well. These wines are best bought in the most recent vintages. They include: Alsatian Pinot Blancs, Côtes du Rhône, Muscadet, Bardolino, Valpolicella and inexpensive Spanish Rioja and California Zinfandel. (Also: we do not include 1984 because except for Bordeaux and California reds, the vintage is not recommended.)